Your Money
Secure It! Don't Risk It!!

Your Money
Secure It! Don't Risk It!!

The Essential Guide to *Play . . . Not Work* During Your Retirement Years

David Reindel

ISBN: Softcover 978-1-5035-8160-9
       eBook   978-1-5035-8158-6

Printed in the United States of America by BookMasters, Inc
Ashland OH
August 2015

Rev. date: 07/21/2015

To order additional copies of this book, contact:
Xlibris
1-888-795-4274
www.Xlibris.com
Orders@Xlibris.com
716721

Table of Contents

FOREWORD

By
Paul Cravinho

(A few Words About Paul Cravinho from Author David Reindel)

*I*N *APRIL, 2015, on the day Paul Cravinho presented the Foreword to this book, the DOW was going through another downturn, down 287 points at that particular moment in the trading day, with the S&P down 20 and other indexes on the slide – all having to do with yet another panic over another possible default in Greece, among other issues driving the market further into negative territory.*

Paul Cravinho is a veteran investor who "tries not to pay much attention to all that." I am proud and pleased to have Paul's Foreword in this book because, ironically, he is not all about just annuities. Paul has his annuities, of course, but he can afford to go into other directions as well.

Paul has options because, among other reasons, he studied and purchased annuities through me. For anyone in the market considering another look at the safe-harbor zone of retirement, Paul is a good example of someone who is currently in the market, with firm footing in the kinds of planning methods I'm about to present in this book.

Why? . . . Because he and his wife of 50 years live a nice, retired life in a beautiful little cove on the Atlantic Ocean near my office, in Mystic, and they want to keep it that way.

Paul spent much of his working career as a probate judge and as a professional tax accountant with 160 clients and 15 small businesses in his practice. Although he left the full-time working world in 2007, he still maintains contact with his loyal clients, still enjoys playing the market and he still has his real estate holdings while holding notes attached to several private mortgages, all of which bring in a tidy income. The long story made short: Paul knows how to make money, but he also knows to keep his 'safe-money' out of hot water. Paul accordingly includes annuities in his mix of assets.

I'll let Paul Cravinho take it from here:

****

"I pay attention to stocks that are primarily in the biotech group," Paul says, "so I'm still in the market. In fact, my broker likes to say that I've put together my own kind of personalized mutual fund. What he means is that I've assembled my own group of 20 different kinds of stocks, from Verizon to Exxon to shares in my 'bio-tech' group, a kind of mutual-fund style of market investment. Last year the fair-market value for my group of securities was up around 12 %.

"Then Dave Reindel contacted me with news that one of my Fixed Index Annuities was up 8%. Considering that this annuity has no risk of losing money, that's pretty great in comparison. So, with Dave I've purchased four different annuities through the years, and all of them are indexed annuities because, I am still able to participate in the market –when the market is up. When the market is down, it's still great because I know my annuities won't lose any money!

"With Dave's annuities it's always a win-win situation.

"My wife and I live near a casino and Dave always reminds us that we can head for the roulette table in any casino, put $100 down on black and spin the wheel. As Dave says, "In roulette, if you bet on the black and it hits on red, you lose. When you're in annuities, if you bet on black and the annuity goes into the black you win. However, if the ball drops into the red, you still win with the fixed indexed annuity because you can't lose your money . . . and yet *you still get to stay in the game*!

"Dave told us in the beginning that his annuities would work this way, and that's the way it has been ever since. Today the market is down, and it could be back up tomorrow. There are factors that could cause it to go down again The feds are going to raise interest rates, for one example, probably in June or maybe September (2015), which could send the market into another downward slide.

"Dave's annuities give us a feeling of steady growth with a sense of security. When the market's good, we see straight gains of 3% or 4% - in some of our annuities - over a 10-year period. A 30% to 40% increase over 10 years, which is outstanding, especially when you consider that you can't lose when the market tanks.

"But the real value is found in what Dave tells all of his clients: *'It's protection of your principal that you should be concerned about.'*

"For many people their principal is the last ticket on the train. You can't afford to have your $100,000 principal fluctuating between $50,000 and $100,000 all the time. What you want to do is to maintain that $100,000 principal and make $2,000 here, $2,000 there. In some years, with a fixed index annuity, you might not make anything but the next year you might make $4,000 or $5,000 . . . *and that is the way to grow income.*

"Personally speaking, we'll probably use Dave's annuities as a legacy for our children and grandchildren. This is definitely something to think about for people who are financially stable. While Dave's annuities can be part of a plan with other investments, mine are for the purpose of inheritance. We don't need our annuities as income at all because we have enough from my dividends, pensions and social security. So, why not let those annuities keep building a legacy for our children and grandchildren? You can use annuities, particularly indexed annuities, in all kinds of ways, but this works best for us. Dave always looks at each individual and how to get the best outcome for that person.

"Our annuities will be payable to independent trusts, which we created in order to have the income pay into the trusts, and then eventually pay out to our beneficiaries. Those pay-outs will be tax-advantaged. Some people need to consider the current $5.4 million federal estate tax exemption limit. In Connecticut, we also face the state's $2 million estate tax exemption limit. An annuity strategy involving trusts can help many people in this situation. Serving as a probate judge for 25 years, I was in touch with many estate attorneys through the years, I've seen all these methods work one way or another, and I've put some of those strategies to good use for our financial security.

"But in the end, it all boils down to just one thing: *piece of mind*.

"My wife ensures that 'piece-of-mind' is maintained at the top of our priority list, by keeping our assets more on the conservative side rather than in risk. However, I gamble on the stock market and I like to play it more with my gut. It is the perfect balance! In addition, we have our fixed indexed annuities – you might call them our backup plan.

"I'll never forget the way things were back in 2008, when a lot of people liquidated all their securities. Although you might think I would have cashed out too, I held firm on the shares I had. When the market rebounded, it came back to a greater degree than before it fell. I'd learned to be patient rather than react back in 1987, when stocks fell through the floor during a big market crash. Back then, the market recovered with some stocks going up three to five times their value after they'd hit bottom. The lesson here is that too many people play on panic, which is the craziest way to play the stock market. In other words, if you are going to have stocks, you have to be able to afford to hang on, which is another reason to have annuities in your back-up plan.

"I value Dave's approach because he consistently offers a broad spectrum of advice, which includes not only annuities and life insurance, but also taxes and Social Security. He has past experience in real estate and other areas, which has given him extensive experience in the financial world.

"His advice is not limited to handling large amounts of money. He presents valuable information in his Social Security seminars. Dave has an exceptional grasp of the subject, telling people why it's so important to wait past the early retirement age, if you can, to get another 8 percent return on the money rather than take it at 62. He provides detailed scenarios about, say, taking a wife's Social Security base (benefit) while the husband lets his benefit grow.

"Dave provides financial advice to a broad range of individuals, in various financial situations, and he is held in high esteem within our community.

"My wife especially likes the way Dave takes great care to plan a retirement for every individual - with a unique plan made just for them, based on their personal situation. When we first decided to get some outside advice, my wife was very skeptical about going to another financial planner, but my grandfather always said, "There's always somebody who knows better than you about what you know.

"Yet, the thing that made us decide to go with Dave was honesty. We started with one annuity through Dave and what he projected would happen actually happened! So, we bought another annuity, and, again, things turned out just as he'd said. Then we bought another, and another, and another – and each time Dave's savvy advice never failed. I've been in the investment world a long time and I can say that this is not always the case with every advisor.

"Here's something else that may be unique among people in Dave's business: If he thinks something about a program is going to become less than favorable, he'll call me and suggest getting out of one thing and into another, which never costs us money because he always finds a bonus attached, or some other way to pay off the surrender value.

"For this and many other reasons, I highly recommend Dave Reindel to all of my clients. The clients I have to this day *still* have Dave Reindel as a financial planner.

"As for me, I'm just happy to be alive and well, retired and living the life. Good health is all you need. Everything else is secondary. I have triumphed over difficult challenges with my own health, and I expect to live to be a hundred. Longevity is in my family, and I know the best is yet to come! All I have to do, now, is to find out how to buy the moon and a rainbow, for my wife. Those are the only things I haven't bought her and, well, once you get her the rainbow, you know how it goes: then you've got to buy her the moon. I have the rest of my life to figure it out."

INTRODUCTION

. . . To a Way of Life

Retirement is all about play . . . not work!

IN THE UPCOMING pages of this book you will discover some of the most important information you will ever find when it comes to your future retirement lifestyle. But first I'd like to share my own story, which made me an authority on growing and preserving incomes for literally hundreds of clients. They now live their retirement dreams, but it didn't happen overnight.

The essential topics in this book are of vital importance to everyone in America today. When prospective clients visit my office, they immediately realize that, in a way, I'm already 'living the dream' myself. I live and work in one of the most beautiful areas of the nation, overlooking the breathtaking shores and beaches of the Atlantic Ocean around Mystic, Connecticut. My clients hail from just about everywhere, from nearby Westerly, Rhode Island to San Diego, California, and all points in between.

Yet, they all came to me through the years for one, primary purpose: to create a solid reliable retirement plan with income that cannot be outlived. They wanted safety of principal guaranteed. They also wanted the ultimate guarantee, the most important commodity one could ever know: *peace of mind*. You should know that they now enjoy all of the above and more.

Let's talk about who I am, and how I can make a difference in your retirement lifestyle!

The 'Why' Behind My Business Model

I could have easily opened an office in New York City, which is not too far from here but far enough. I suppose I could have frantically built up a big Manhattan-based practice with lots of people working for me, but I took another road.

I chose long ago to instead create a friendly, low-key office in one of the most beautiful spots in southern New England. I'm a stone's throw from the famous Mystic Harbor and everything you have heard about that magical setting is true: it is a wonderful place. Here, in this relaxed setting, my clients can drop in anytime and chat, and many do. You can see why.

This is just a great place to be! It's also a very fitting, appropriately inspiring place to talk about retirement. People who want to risk all on the S&P would probably rather hang out with a Wolf on Wall Street. In my office, we protect and preserve retirement dreams. Why? Because *retirement should be all about play, not work!*

Tossing and turning all night with nagging worries over market risk sounds like "work" to me! If you agree, we're on the same page! I also think that my office at #1 Allen Street in Mystic also affects the way I do business: personal, patient, willing to give clients all the time they need to stretch out, mull things over, take their time . . . in order to fully realize the kind of retirement plan they not only *can* begin to implement, but the kind of lifestyle they will truly *enjoy*. Again, it's all about "peace of mind" more than flashy wealth. I'm talking about the truly rewarding experience of a life well lived, rather than the anxious pursuit of an image sustained by risk.

This is the place to contemplate what life is all about in retirement. It is the kind of place where the concept of "rewards" have more to do with keeping up with friends and family, taking long walks on the beach, maybe taking up creative projects you have always wanted to try. In fact, I'll introduce you to a couple of people who took this approach. I'll also show you how you may have more potential wealth and a much brighter future than you might have ever dreamed.

But I don't make promises. I'm not in the business of weaving unrealistic dreams. We take a look at who you are and what you have, then we often re-build a plan with the best future possible based on real, substantive numbers, not the "projections" of risk.

Some might say I'm a different kind of financial planner for all of the reasons stated above. But it all came about because of who I was in the beginning. I learned the true value of a dollar very early on. I accordingly developed a passion to protect the dollars of others. Later on in the book, I will share a complete run-down of my professional career, but for now, I just want to share a bit about who I am based on where I've been in my life. After all, if you were asked to share all the intimate details of your finances, and things about your family and lifestyle as they relate to your future in retirement, wouldn't you like to know who you're working with? Of course.

I live beside the sea every day, but it wasn't always like this. In fact, I'm living the realization of a lifelong dream and it didn't come easily. I came from modest means so I've always had a job. I had an ambitious paper route as a kid, as a teenager I worked long hours in a shoe store with as much overtime as I could get. Later on, and through my college years, I worked with dedication and much personal satisfaction as a counselor in a summer camp, helping kids and discovering a new world, myself, along the way.

Turning Dreams to Reality

My years at the camp inspired my 'ocean dream.' My ocean dream drove my will to succeed. Somewhere along the way, I bought a motorcycle. If you have ever ridden a motorcycle you know that once you really master the machine, you feel like you're flying, and "flying" along on my motorcycle inspired me to take to the skies, so I joined the Civil Air Patrol, which further inspired me to consider a career with the U.S. Air Force . . . but something brought me back to earth.

I think it had to do with the way I was able to help those kids and others along the way.

Instead, I attended Central Connecticut State University where I picked up an avid interest in mathematics. As I built a strong background as an academically educated mathematician, I kept working at the summer camp, donating my preseason weekends to mowing lawns, cleaning cabins and following a punch list of to-do items to get everything ready for the campers. Looking back, this is where I really developed the ability to listen to others.

Thanks to that experience, when I entered the insurance business I was able to place the needs of my clients ahead of my own from day one. If someone wants to succeed in the insurance business, they must take a genuine interest in others. You must care as much about others as you would about yourself. After all, my job is all about *protecting* someone else's life savings in retirement. It's not about me: This kind of outlook might not be important in every trade, but I consider it essential in mine.

After college and as a very young man of 24, I founded, owned and operated a property and casualty insurance business. I was always able to maintain a position among the company's top-producers as I do today, but it all began back then because I discovered a fundamental element that would lead to success: I took a conservative approach to planning the futures of my clients. I've been in this business for more than 35 years, I have continued to study and improve my knowledge, but I've always maintained that conservative, risk-averse, fundamental approach when caring for my clients and their future in retirement.

Multi-Tasking: Your Insurance RIA

Unlike many in my industry, while being fully educated and licensed in all-things-insurance, I also studied and became a licensed Registered Investment Advisor, which allows me to address market issues and securities. You might ask why, since I believe so firmly in aspects of insurance-based financial planning for retirees. Well, think about it: Most people are going to go to someone like myself with all sorts of "financial baggage" tied up in risky, market investments. Without my RIA and other securities designations, I would be legally prevented from discussing those market investments. I'll talk about this later, but I think anyone can understand why an RIA is essential for the way I do business.

I also firmly believe in the power of giving back to the community, *without* using charity as a means-to-an-end to get more business. If my charities lead to new business, I put the proceeds back into the charities. I started the Reindel Heritage Foundation many years ago to help church mentoring programs for everyone from needy kids from abusive homes to released prisoners who deserve a helping hand to get back on their feet. I have contributed quite heavily to everything from the national organization, Autism Speaks, to a homeless shelter, to a program for Ethiopian famine relief.

I *have* learned much from my charity work, although I can't count it in terms of dollars or sales. Giving back helps me continue to reinforce my life-long belief in how *not to sell*.

Anti-Sales

I guess I'd call it "anti-sales." Strangely enough, to excel in sales I decided not to "sell" in the strict sense of the word. I call it "service." Sometimes you need to give things away to get things in return. I build my business relationships by freely providing knowledge, with or without a dollar of profit as an end result. You'll see what I mean in later chapters.

I also love to teach and share information. I love to answer questions because I know my stuff and I love what I do, and I spend more time getting to know people than I do cashing paychecks.

Forget about sales-persuasion/high-pressure sales "techniques." If you come into my office, I simply want to get to know you. The rest just naturally falls into place. If we build a relationship, it's because I get to know you and you know me. That's the only way to create a truly workable plan for your future. It's not about selling you something.

The old "sales pitch" just doesn't work for me. It never did. Instead, I give you the facts. You consider the facts and make your own informed decisions.

Non-selling means fact-finding and, in my line of work, it leads to safe, reliable, income-based retirement planning—that's me. And in the end, I feel great about what we've done because I know how well my plan will work for you. Also, I get paid for it! What could be better?

Making a Difference

Later on in this book, I will go into detail about the many ways I've challenged "standard" practice among insurance companies entrenched in their own agendas. I've helped create more consumer-friendly products, among other things, explaining that it would improve the relationships agents have with their prospects (of course!). Companies have often come to me asking how I became so successful and I've shared the above with them (and more). Unfortunately, some carriers and their sales executive still don't get it. Others have. In fact, this industry has come a long way in the right direction since I was new to the business.

Insurance products have vastly improved since then. Presentations and illustrations have become far more detailed and professional. Customers today know more about what they're getting into as opposed to what was disclosed in the past. We have a ways to go, but we're getting there. Meanwhile, millions of investors have come running since the Great Recession to a new generation of solid retirement planning products. We're also generating many more, genuinely motivated *safe-retirement advocates* than ever before. In other words, things I (and others like me) have been saying are catching on. People want to keep their savings safe and secure. But they want to take advantage of ways to grow their savings, too, and the "smart-money" insurance carrier has been listening.

The Upside Spin: Beware

A bull market, like the one we're in at this writing in mid-2015, may create the impression that upside potential will never end. At a time like this, financial spin-doctors actually try to make it seem like diverting money from risk is a risk in itself. What? Okay, you're risking the loss of some risk-based opportunity, but a market drop takes your money down, all the same. But human nature is what it is. Caught up in upside "market excitement" (greed), our fears tend to fade until we see the need for temperance, once again. By then, it's often too late. Mountains of retirement savings have been lost.

Since my earliest beginnings in this business, I knew I would have to guide my clients through rough waters. Back then, I'd heard every story about the great crash of 1929, and I was determined to prepare myself, and my clients, for the worst.

At times like this, I sometimes find myself having to remind people that up-markets *do not* live forever. But make no mistake: After surviving some of the worst market declines in our lifetime, my retired clients have been able to recover their losses without having to go back to work, and anyone who went through the Crash of '08 knows the truth: You can't replace preservation of principal as the foundation of peace-of-mind. This is why my end of the financial service industry has literally exploded in popularity.

I offer *guaranteed income* and *principal.* I also offer ways to participate in market-*related* earnings through shared interest, also known as value-credits, which allow my clients to reap the *rewards* of upside markets *without the risk.* They cannot lose the money they make. They cannot lose the principal they begin with. Instead, they gain value as they pile on new income.

In short, I am in the business of providing all of the above through annuities. . . . But not just *any* old species of annuity. I'll explain. In this book I will also share much more – far more – about other ways to add to my strategies with guaranteed income you might have in your hands right now. I'll show you how to maximize what you have without spending another dime to do it.

But I will ask you to do one thing for me as you read this book: Even in this wildly, dangerously, soaring market environment, I want for you to consider one thing: Right now, please consider trading *risk* for the *rewards* of having financial guarantees for the rest of your life. I will provide a wealth of related knowledge in this book that you can literally take to the bank.

Like many reading these words, I, too, am a so-called "boomer." I know where you have been and I listen to your retirement fears every day. Let's start to put those fears to rest, shall we? I know . . . you've been through some tumultuous cultural, economic, and political turmoil. We've been through it together from Vietnam in the '60s, through 9/11, and on to the prime mortgage meltdown and Great Recession of 2008-2009. Now we're holding on to a mind-numbing surge on the S&P, which seemed to have no limit through the end of 2014. Today, we're still in the rarified atmosphere of 18,000-plus on the DOW, and that's why we need to pay attention.

. . . Your *'Mindset Reset'*

We need to take charge at a time like this. We need to do a recession-survivor's *"Mindset Reset."* We need to establish some real traction in the direction of guarantees for our retirement lifestyles and this should be a no-brainer for most.

I talk to people from our generation every day and these people are rightly concerned about their retirement. Forget about those dreamy brokerage ads showing rich retirees floating into the sunset on 40-foot yachts! Most boomers worry constantly about hanging on financially in their declining years. We'll talk about the hurdles we must all carefully consider in the coming decade. For now, though, I want you to take the helm and take charge of your own destiny. Do not rely on some company 401k advisor for direction. Do not expect a broker to keep you from falling through the cracks in the next crash.

You must see yourself in the leadership role of your own destiny, and I will show you how to do just that! My business is all about guaranteed financial independence, largely through insurance-based financial planning, but I have a level of flexibility mostly lacking among others in my industry. But to work with me, you must set your financial peace of mind as a primary goal. You need a Mindset-Reset.

Clients come into my office all the time immersed in what basically amounts to risk addiction. If this sounds like you, no worries, you're not alone. You just need to let me re-adjust your vision a bit and the content of this book is a good start. Your victory lap will happen the day you walk out of my office feeling re-born with a new sense of life-long security.

And here's something uncommon among people in my business, because most aren't qualified to pull it off: *After* my formerly risk-addicted clients have established a strong foundation of guaranteed income – *after that* – I might just find them enough random dough to fling at the market wall, if that's what they want after I show them the amazing, value-added features in my guaranteed-income plans. But many won't. Once they see the truth, they get it.

I often work with certain, highly effective, consumer-friendly Fixed Indexed Annuity products. I can offer related, strategic instruments as well, some of which protect savings against long-term illness. Social Security maximization is another, vitally important issue and if you haven't considered the many built-in secrets of SSI (Social Security Income), you will find everything you need to know in this book before you come in to meet with me.

For now, I'm excited to hear what *you* have to say. After reading this book, I want you to step back a minute and – this might sound strange – but *remember the summer of 2008*. That's right, the summer of '08! Why the summer of 2008? That was before the crash, when people thought things were "fine." They were, compared to the horrendous, catastrophic season to come, when things would take a turn for the worse, especially for people mired in risk.

That's my point: *Nobody* knew what was coming.

CHAPTER ONE

The Wages of **Risk** *. . .*
How to Avoid Financial Disaster

I F YOU HAD no other perspective than a tunnel-view of current markets and economies, you might assume a soaring market would spell unending prosperity. You might even be tempted to add more risk to your financial future, because runaway bull-markets might tempt even the more prudent investor. At this writing, we've seen the S&P index soar to unheard of new heights. We've listened to all sorts of people brag about their latest killings on Wall Street.

But let me tell you about bull markets and runaway enthusiasm. It's like a never-ending story. Bull and bear markets each have a beginning, a middle, and end, just like all stories. When the horror story of the Great Recession finally ground to a bitter end, the average investor had been hardened by a season of hard knocks after the DOW came crashing down. These days, you can ask them what they think as the DOW soars and dips in the rarified environs of 18,000 and above. They know better. They have achieved the wisdom of experience. They now have most of their money in a fortress of income guarantees, with principal that can never evaporate with the next dive on Wall Street.

Yes, some have reached into what I call their "red" wallet. The "red wallet" is where they stash the money they know they shouldn't risk. This is the sacred cow of core 'principle,' the fail-safe money put to work in ways designed to provide guaranteed income for life. Some have risked this kind of money against my best advice and long experience, so I have devised even more flexible plans, which I will talk about later on. But first and absolutely foremost, if you want to work with me, you must know that I am a mathematician. I am a life-long student of the hard realities of numbers and economics. I'm talking about the entire, "world history" of economies, not just the short-term 'euphoria' triggered by reactionary American bull markets. With that perspective, I can safely say, "Yes, we can take advantage of bull markets." But you must know how to participate *without* risk.

Impossible Made Possible

"Impossible," you say? I answer in the affirmative: Yes, it IS possible. You *can* MAKE money in a bull market *without risk*. You can do it without losing money, without risking a cent of your life savings. In this book I will show you how.

In this book, I will share secrets intended to help almost every American, people of all walks of life who want to retire with peace of mind. In this book, you will get the facts and substance, not just gauzy promises, as presented through techniques and financial instruments that will change your life . . . the minute you hit the "go" button.

No matter what kind of market we're seeing at any given time, the trick is to avoid risking a red cent as you make your money grow . . . even as you take income. Yes, it can be done! You can actually *earn* while you *turn* your savings into monthly paychecks. I can show you how to achieve the seemingly impossible combination of gain without loss.

Again, the solutions I'm about to share in this book did not appear overnight. It took years of research and experience. Yet, my methods have been proven time and again, in market corrections, in overnight "adjustments" turning billions of investor assets to dust. My plans have survived the most catastrophic financial markets known to humankind since the Great Depression, which, in fact, was triggered by the stock market crash of 1929. Not so differently than the Crash of 2008, although we had a few chocks in the bursting dike, this time around.

Our more recent economic tsunami began to thunder inland around 2007. Investors at the time were in ecstatic over a market characterized by under-powered shares with high-powered prices, and quick profits with things like bundled real estate/mortgage investments. Big killings were sometimes realized overnight until the dawning of a horrible reality: October 2008. This is when we saw the collapse of bundled, mortgage-backed securities, which begat waves of failure among financial institutions. If it began on Wall Street, the red-tide of economic collapse swept worldwide. The fall was so pervasive, and precipitous, it took down more than just the world of stocks, bonds and mutual funds. The Great *Recession* of 2008-2009 took down entire *industries*, some of which never quite recovered. Much of the publishing and newspaper industries were swept up in the financial tsunami . . . and never quite recovered.

Neither did millions upon millions of retirement portfolios. Average Americans saw half their savings go down the tubes in an afternoon. You were probably there. I know I was. I knew the economy was in trouble and that the market was due to fall. Yet, like most people in the financial world, I had no idea *just how far* the pendulum would swing.

A host of former job descriptions simply never came back. As companies grasped for any financial life-vest available, workloads were consolidated, jobs were cut and outsourced. Fewer workers took on more work. Corporate profits began to revive but ever greater numbers of former employees were left in the streets – including pre-retirees on the eve of receiving the ill-fated gold watch. Millions of boomers were cut loose and left in the cold during what should have been their peak earning years, the critical, sensitive earning years leading to the door of retirement. Careers vanished along with retirement savings. Retirement dreams were swept into the abyss. Few escaped "The Wrath of the Math." That's what I call it. Some of us saw it coming: Way too many market shares were based on numbers that simply did not add up. Again, I knew it, I made sure my clients were safe and sound. None of them suffered the horrific consequences of risk as the financial outcome of 2008 began to take its toll. In the after math, however, a positive silver lining began to emerge.

All of a sudden, more and more people – and their advisors - were suddenly open to the kind of risk-free market participation I'd been advocating all along. A nation of investors had grown weary of catastrophic market loss.

Yet, those are the wages of risk. I will illustrate how the numbers really play out as we focus on safeguards and a fortress of future solutions. But first, let's take a closer look at something I consider almost incredible. I say, "Almost," because I've learned much about human nature and money. At times like this, the greed-factor becomes all-important, over-powering and seemingly unstoppable. Then fear sets in. Then reality. But that's another story.

Let's look at today: Investors who lost boatloads of cash are the same ones who felt obliged to go after the same market that sank them in the last crash. Irony, irony! I talk to people like this every day. At first they felt they had to stay in the game to recover their losses. That done, they now feel forced to stay embedded in risk to make up for lost time, and add – desperately – to the plus-side of the ledger . . . before it's too late. That's the really twisted part of the tale! Having been through the "lost decade" (I'll explain), they *know for a fact* that everything will eventually come crashing down again. So, there they are again, tossing and turning at night, pounding digits in their cell phones by day, trying to reach their brokers . . . hanging on every word, every time the numbers slip and slide.

"So, the economy is improving," people like to say. Yes, ever since the Federal Reserve 'stimulation programs' began, the US economy has been steadily improving. Interest rates in the US have remained artificially low as the fed prints more money until we all recover financially, or so goes the conventional wisdom. In truth, we're strapped to a train of debt, and this train is picking up steam. I'm happy to see a rebounding economy, believe me. Housing, overall employment and key manufacturing sectors have been running in the black – even as the DOW and S&P have continued to climb to unprecedented heights.

So, why have respected observers from Robert Shiller to Harry Dent warned that a market "correction" is not just imminent, it is long overdue?

We have all welcomed relief from a punishing recession. Yet, experts at top financial organizations like Gradient Investments noted in February, 2015, that a relentlessly bullish forecast had begun to change. They called for a "flattish" domestic stock market in early 2015 as investors would digest strong gains of prior years. At the same time, however, the US Purchasing Manager's Index indicated a slowdown, for the first time in several years. Other indicators called for an impending pause in the heretofore relentless action on Wall Street – all of which turned out to be numerically prophetic: the DOW and S&P slipped considerably in April, 2015.

The Clock is Ticking

Some believe the market is in for a more significant correction at some point and, at this writing, energy stocks have been falling as oil prices plummet. *Forbes* magazine recently declared that the market is approximately 65 percent overvalued – the result of "irrational" enthusiasm, they say. As if we trench-survivors don't already know! We've been here before! The gun is loaded. Too many investors are playing a dangerous game of Risk Roulette and I think they know it. But they can't seem to stop, for fear of losing "market opportunities." That's the language of risk: "losing market opportunities." Broker's call *that* risk! Hmm, you *stay in risk* to avoid losing money *at risk* so as not *to risk losing* money *at risk*. This is the "pretzel logic" I describe in all my books.

Later in this book, I'll revisit some of those who were "in the trenches," who show how they survived by avoiding risk, while millions of other lost their retirement lifestyles in the crash. I'll share a couple of those stories to remind us that economies are all about cycles.

I've passed along the predictions above, not to sound dire warnings of doom-and-gloom. That is not my intention, not at all. I just want to remind everyone of hard numbers and statistical, historical fact. When it comes to the catastrophic market collapse, well, *these things happen.* I'm trying to sound a wake-up call when it comes to risk. None of my current clients need this kind of wake-up call. They're survivors. They've been there, shocked by the cold-water slap of a sudden drop on the S&P at one time or another.

Others were able to escape the Great Crash, but only *just in time.* They came to me at the 11th hour. Thanks to a "timely" decision to go with my risk-free alternatives, these people were able to play golf through the last recession - while their friends went back to work, as front-door greeters in big-box chain stores.

The funny thing about incoming risk and loss is the ever-changing disguise it might wear on the approach. We never know exactly how, or when, the market-emperor's cloak will fall away and disclose the 'real' numbers. Only at the last second before the gong, at the end of daily trading, do we sometimes discover de-stabilizing factors behind over-valued markets.

Numerous national and international headlines have warned, for example, that the cumulative effects of sluggish European markets will impact global markets. GDP growth throughout Europe has been stagnating around zero for quite some time, while proposed solutions include stimulation programs via lowered interest rates, which may provide too little, too late. A Greek-socialist party swept recent elections with promises to reverse current government spending practices which, according to some observers, would plunge that nation into bankruptcy. The sudden emergence of such trends can have a chilling effect on Wall Street and other global trading exchanges. And by April, 2015, analysts were worried that Greece would indeed default on its obligations . . . too little, too late.

Risk itself is a chameleon with unlimited ways of obscuring the big picture for risk-immersed investors. As some observers point out, relations between the U.S. and India seem to be improving, thus indicating positive forces for the currently stable US market. Others contend that an overriding volatility is in the air. Yet, volatility is almost always "in the air," somewhere, isn't it? Market volatility, like political volatility is, in fact, not always a bad thing for the highly informed. Market volatility can be a boon to highly informed investors. Yet, those investors are different than most of the rest of us. They can also *afford to juggle risk and loss against projected gains.* They include institutions that invest over a 100-year timeline. Time is perpetually on their side, *as it is with the most powerful insurance organizations, some of which have been around for more than a century.*

I am going to show you how *you* can share in some of the profits of the "highly informed." In this book, I will show you how you can do this without risking *one thin dime* of your own principal. While we examine risk in this chapter, this book is really focused on *reward* – so stay with me.

First, we must accept the fact that the great majority of American retirees have no remaining time for recovery from major losses on the DOW and S&P. Like it or not, retirees today are in a complex race against things like inflation and longevity, meaning, it no longer works to just sit back on a mattress stuffed with cash and let the world go by. Risk today is different than it was 60 years ago, or even 30 years ago. It's not all about avoiding the next stock market somersault. Now we must factor in a new host of realities including a highly inter-connected global family of market gains and losses.

The Risk of 'Mattress-Money'

This fundamental shift in has not been lost on millions of pre-retirees and people in retirement. Since the crash of '08, many retirees have even become overly enthusiastic savers-turned-hoarders. This, unfortunately, may present a degree of risk in itself because these people will eventually discover that cash sitting under the mattress can be challenged by inflation and other factors. Luckily, we haven't seen any serious inflation growth so far. But we have seen persistently sluggish interest rates attached to instruments like money markets and bank CDs – the modern-day haven of sidelined "mattress-money."

In short, the term "risk" isn't necessarily tied to runaway securities markets. Some people risk financial erosion simply by leaving cash on the sidelines, only to wake up one day, smell the coffee and dive into the market to recover. That's where a certain kind of disguised risk kicks in: People suddenly find themselves following the advice of commission-happy advisors chasing investments with uncertain outcomes. In this situation, investments are made in markets where both investors and their advisors have little or no control of the outcome.

Many people in this situation have no room for failure. They've suffered the repeated loss of assets from an insidiously corrosive set of variables, dating back as far as a late '90s drop in the S&P. That's how far the corrosive effects on a portfolio can really be!

Taking that in stride, the same investors were whacked again, and again. Their investments suffered when a tech bubble burst in 2001, which triggered another market crash . . . followed by another market drop after the 9/11 terrorists attacks. When immersed in risk, both the quality of your lifestyle, and market volatility, dance together in the shadow of running bulls and bears. Some people love the dance, staying late at the party as markets rise and fall. They always have and always will, but direct market investing means constant risk. To drink from this kind of punch bowl requires acceptance of periodic losses, which – as we all know – can be considerable. So, how, and when, do we cash out of the casino and sober up?

Sobering Truth

The sobering truth: Most pre-retirees and retirees can no longer afford to play. A recent study by the Employee Benefit Research Institute revealed that a huge percentage of Americans - including 44% of those born between 1948 and 1978 known as 'Baby Boomers' and 'Generation X' - will never see an adequate level of retirement income. Here's why:

They gambled retirement portfolios before and even during the last recession and they're at it again. Yes, the market took off after the notorious 2008-09 bear market. By 2013, it had risen more than 100%. Some analysts expected a correction, or at least a cooling effect in advance of predicted inflationary spikes and tax hikes. Investors had indeed yanked more than $280 billion out of the mutual fund market. The fed kept interest rates low. Investors had pumped more than $800 billion into bonds with less volatility but lower earnings to match.

Re-thinking 401Ks

Another segment of the U.S. workforce has, meanwhile, remained committed to defined contribution plans including 401k plans, which essentially lock money into the risk-laden system of market-driven securities. This makes sense when employees are younger - and if employers offer to match funds put into the plan. But not all employers offer matching contributions these days, we've all seen what can happen to a 401k when the market takes a dive, and, as we near retirement, we have little or no time to recover from severe market corrections.

It thus becomes imperative to *re-think* the way we invest in the future: Maxing out a 401k plan becomes a risk in itself as we pass a certain age. This is precisely when it becomes critically important to re-assess and reset your retirement strategy. Yes, it can be a time to diversify, but not in the traditional sense of so-called "asset allocation," meaning a diversified mix of securities, IRAs and 401ks.

CHAPTER TWO

Treasury and the Retirement Crisis . . . The New "Default" Solution

I N THIS ENVIRONMENT, even the U.S. Department of the Treasury very recently recognized the need for retirees to *diversify-away* from traditional 401K planning methods. In October, 2014, the treasury department actually came out and encouraged sponsors of defined benefit plans (pensions) to *"include deferred-income annuities"* as a kind of *"default investment"* - if in compliance with qualification rules.

Reading between the lines, this was a big step for the traditionally neutral Fed, but after watching the effects of the '08 - '09 crash on retirement plans at the time, Treasury officials all but pointed the way toward reduced risk and volatility for retirees. In other words, "risk" is on the Fed radar – they *get it*. Without risk-mitigation becoming a major part of the U.S. financial landscape, millions of seniors will be in serious trouble in the coming years. If this happens, many sectors of the national economy will be affected and this is of much concern to treasury officials.

For starters, a good number of boomers could transition from being powerful consumers to becoming a mass of people dependent on government programs . . . and we're just getting started. Visionary government analysts understandably hope to inspire new retirement planning tactics across the board. And guess where they hope to find a solution: remember the term *"deferred income annuities"* above? That's right: annuities. Annuities provide income deferred, or delayed, until a future point in time. My annuities allow your money to increase that income exponentially. Above all, such annuities provide certain *guarantees* in retirement, which is something neither company IRA/401K programs can do. With the once tried-and-true company pension vanishing quickly into history, Americans must adopt a new, financial roadmap to retirement.

Treasury Secretary Senior Advisor J. Mark Iwry came right out and said it in a recent media release:

"As boomers approach retirement and life expectancies increase," Iwry declared, "income annuities can be an important planning tool for a secure retirement." Also Deputy Assistant Secretary for Retirement and Health Policy, Iwry went on to add that "Treasury is working to expand the availability of retirement income options for working families. By encouraging the use of income annuities, today's guidance can help retirees protect themselves from outliving their savings."

"Protect" themselves? Did you catch that? . . . Protect retirees from what? . . . Market risk, that's what! And that powerful statement above comes direct from government sanctioned expertise.

Securities advisors have long echoed sentiments of investors like billionaire Warren Buffet, who at one point insisted that stocks could be a better bet than 'sidelined' cash, bonds, gold and other so-called "safe" assets. This might be appropriate advice for those who can afford to play the market indefinitely. As indicated earlier, these individuals can leverage risk and budget for the inevitable financial whack. But most people can't. That's the problem. Yet, a disturbing number of small players have been accordingly lured back into the game, not fully understanding what I perceive to be the meaning of such advice. In a way, I agree with Warren Buffet: You cannot leave your life savings stuffed into a comparative institutional mattress. On the other hand, most of us must, in my opinion, dramatically mitigate risk while using alternative strategies. My strategies offer what I consider the ultimate mitigation of risk. But some people *still don't get it*.

The traumatic shock that led many into risk-averse investing seems to have worn off, at a time when market observers wonder just how much higher this dizzying market can continue to rise. We've seen the scallop effect in recent months. A fall-off in European markets led to decreased use of transportation, which triggered lower demand for fuel, which created a dip in energy stocks. That's all it took. This is how risk works. One event triggers another.

Risky Longevity

Is living too long risky, too? It can be, unfortunately, not that I'd want to see anyone go out and jump off a bridge, at age 89. Heaven forbid!

The much discussed, so-called "longevity risk" phenomenon has less to do with the mechanics of financial instruments, more to do with aging. At a time when inflation kicks into gear, along with taxation to pay for government bailouts during the last recession, and a government "health care-reform" program with untold economic consequences, American retirees will be living longer than ever before – longer, at least, than anyone ever imagined long ago, when pensions and Social Security ruled the day for most retirees.

This simple fact of life - *longer and longer life* - could have a greater impact on aging Americans in the years to come. Most retirees in the 1950s lived until age 68, or so, while many Americans today live well into their 90s, and many 'live well' in the process. This is great for some, but not so great for others. If you have a source of unlimited income for the rest of your life, living a long and 'prosperous' life is a wonderful thing. But what if you run out of money at age 75 and realize that you may need *another 20 more years of income* in retirement?!

Today, many retirement advisors know to tell their already-retired clients to plan on living for another 25 years, or more. Wonderful. But what if you haven't saved enough to live that long? Unfortunately, a massive number of Americans have either lost most of their retirement savings, or they have no savings at all. Since 2008 and the last recession, many have simply given up, essentially banking on a life based on Social Security income, alone.

Today, too many working Americans put retirement-saving in the back seat, spending expendable cash on other things. And, to be fair, many people are *still* climbing out from under a mountain of consumer-debt accumulated during the last recession, which further impacts effective retirement planning. A good many retirees and pre-retirees are still strapped to hefty home mortgages, lines of credit and second mortgages, when a home paid-off and debt-free in retirement was a given 50 years ago. As elder Americans continue to chip-away at things like credit-card balances and auto loans, saving for retirement understandably becomes a distant prospect. Recent studies indicates that more than 60% of Americans have less than $25,000 set aside for retirement, while more than three-quarters of those in this group report serious financial hurdles preventing any kind of savings plan. This is not the result of market risk. This is the consequence of economic wreckage and a struggling recovery. Now add in the effects of pre-mature death of a spouse in retirement, or the impact of even one divorce, early in life, which can have far-reaching consequences on retirement savings. Then consider the effects of more than one divorce, or a divorce occurring later in life, which, disturbingly, is happening with greater frequency these days. This, unfortunately, is part of life in America today. In that such things affect the way I do business, they have become part of life for me.

I have accordingly adjusted my planning strategies to meet the needs of all Americans today – not the faded requirements of dated retirement strategies designed 30 years ago!

Clients sometimes come to me with related financial baggage and I can help. More often than not, assets you may consider less-than-what-they-were can be 'reinvented' into a stable retirement income stream *right now*. It means taking charge, of course. Don't think you can leave those assets sitting around in non-performing instruments: that's the message.

But even worse is the prospect of further economic erosion due to another, so-called market "correction," which can equate to a market "crash" when it affects already impacted assets. So what do you do? The temptation may be to allow such assets to ride the market waves, but this is where discipline becomes so important. Already-reduced resources require even greater special care and handling than other critical assets. I'll show you exactly what I mean in upcoming chapters of this book.

Read Between the Lines and Act . . . Now

Meanwhile, when you hear analysts talk about an "impending Wall Street *correction*," it means that if you are still in risk the market could sink like a millstone attached to your financial neck. When this has happened in the past, almost without exception millions of retirees have lost millions to *billions* of dollars. While younger investors have years and years to recover such losses, elderly investors simply lose income - lots and lots of income - for the rest of their lives. This is because most people in retirement have too little time to recover assets lost in a Wall Street "correction." They lose a significant chunk of lifetime income in the process, income that may never return.

This is what "risk" is all about for retirees and pre-retirees that are similarly affected. A market slide can require radically adjusted retirement lifestyles. If a crash or correction is significant enough, pre-retirees can be forced to keep on working indefinitely; people well into their retirement lives may be forced to go back to work. With a third of the aging U.S. population having little or nothing set aside, the disappearance of the old company pension has left millions of retirees on their own in terms of planning – especially among the boomers. Without knowing about other options, they remain stuck in risk, and that worries me most. Facing the reality of living on half their former income, at best, they may have a lingering mortgage, Medicare supplements and medications that may not be covered by Medicare. Pre-retirees face enormous health care costs as they wallow in the "donut hole," watching monthly health insurance premium overtake last-minute savings strategies. Meanwhile your favorite personal-finance magazine dotes on portrayals of attractive retirees grinning ear-to-ear in a beautiful sunset, as the magazine details their picture-perfect retirement plan. This sells lots of advertising. It makes for a good cover photo. Here's reality: Millions of retirees are struggling at a time when employment opportunities are destined to vanish – let's face it – due to age discrimination and dated skill sets.

Hooked On Risk

Despite the catastrophic effects of the past recession, the loss of careers, and the extinction of former industries as we knew them, millions of pre-retirees still pin their last hopes on the market . . . even as a growing choir of analysts warn about a virtual cavalcade of ongoing "corrections." The occasional market plunge goes with the territory of risk. When stocks, bonds and mutual funds sink like a lead balloon, they may call it an "adjustment." You hear that a lot at this writing: Observers say the market is overdue for an "adjustment." This can mean that Dow is screaming high, that S&P values are over the top, that prices need to level-out to justify values, and so it goes. This is fine, it is what it is - unless you can't afford to take the hit.

Average investors face near-insurmountable odds in today's market when it comes to market timing. Out of desperation to recover past market losses, many revert to former habits, taking market leaps of faith, snapping up "hot" stock tips, betting on blue-chip endurance, relying on the treacherous old law of market averages. And I'm willing to bet that they're hearing basically the same kind of advice they heard in 2007, before global markets collapsed along with domestic and international banking syndicates. The advice of the day: buy, buy, then *"stay the course"* when things get sticky.

However, times have changed. In certain quarters of the financial maze, former risk-adamant advisors now tell their clients to buy into various insurance products. But what kind of products? Do they take a back seat to risk? People in or near retirement should align the old adage about Las Vegas to market risk: The house *always* wins. Brokers make commissions whether or not *you win or lose* in the market. Every time you authorize a trade, every time you act on a stock tip or sell shares, your broker makes money for implementing the move.

For your broker, times of market excitement make money, times of fear make money. Some people run on fear regardless of whether the market is up or down, which is all good for the broker *as long as trading continues.*

I've said it in the pages of books long past: Fear drives irrational market risk. But the *new fear* should be more about running out of money, *not* the fear of missing market opportunities to recover market losses. The latter is what I call 'running the hamster wheel.' Investors jump on the wheel, running essentially in place over a length of time, committed to the same old risk-and-recovery formulas. After the time-proven, numbers-backed reality of the past 13-to-15-year market cycle, we know that running the hamster-race can eventually create *persistent erosion* of retirement dreams.

You, the Future and Your Money

Who knows what the future will bring? I'd like to believe that the market will continue grow with infinite vigor, making everyone a virtual paper millionaire. But we know the truth. The realm of risk and reward on Wall Street is made of cycles, like the rising-falling rhythm of ocean waves, predictable as the incoming-outgoing cycles of the tide. We've seen encouraging economic recovery. We've witnessed spectacular highs on virtually every market index. Yet, Americans still miss the point when it comes to saving for retirement: When it comes to the Casino on Wall Street, *the house giveth, the house taketh away.* Placed on a graph, the illustration of market cycles going back centuries will look like a jig-saw blade. As people struggle to grow money in the market for retirement, they face incoming waves of 'correction' and 'adjustment.'

I've been watching market-based portfolios for decades; they tend to wind up 'beached' at some point because virtually any unsettling force can touch off a rogue wave of selling. World events can trigger a sell-off. The Middle East is in greater turmoil than ever before, which can slow the global flow of oil, which in turn effects almost every corner of our consumer-based economy, including stocks and bonds supported by that economy. *Whatever.*

... Entities structured to survive and prosper in a market-based strategy have an endless supply of time. You don't.

... Try to bank on the rewards of risk as an individual and you risk all.

... Risk does not work over the long haul for most retirees.

The Guaranteed-Money Mandate

Unless you have the financial backing of someone like Bill Gates, you must follow a precisely planned asset-preservation formula, which will be addressed in detail in upcoming chapters of this book. I'm talking about a guaranteed formula – your 'Guaranteed-Money Mandate' - for guaranteed financial success in retirement. Here's how to recognize someone who may talk about retirement safeguards while selling risk: People selling risk like to talk about *estimated* future performance, but you cannot bank on *estimated* market performance without risking horrific consequences. Ask these people if they can "guarantee" income and the safety of your principal and see what happens. If you don't hear an immediate "yes," you're looking at more risk.

Look at past financial debacles affecting millions of people in the U.S. and abroad during the Great Recession and the Great Depression. Yes, such events can and will happen again. But even more likely is the subtle, relentless, agonizing effect of those "minor" market "corrections, dips, declines, adjustments" – all of which will take an untold toll on your bottom line.

However you want to slice the pie, the taste of risk remains the same in the long run: You will lie awake at night in fear of the next financial tsunami.

The Risk of Stagnation

As previously discussed, risk is not Wall Street-exclusive: savings accounts, money markets and CDs earning less-than-zero-percent interest pose the risk of stagnation. Your money might look safe in one of those instruments for now, but what if you happen to live into your 80s and 90s? Can you foretell the future of inflation? They call the 60s the new 40s. The 80s have become the new 60s. That's the problem. With some *$10 trillion in retirement assets* wallowing in accounts earning less-than-zero-percent returns, simple inflation should be a real concern.

Although many people still tremble at memories of the last crash, uncertain about what to do or where to turn, I'm here to say "it's time." It is time to take control of your future. It is time to leave behind the risk of stagnation. It is also time to leave all forms of risk in the dust.

If you find yourself sitting dead-in-the-water on the sidelines with your money, it's time to take control. At the same time, *you need not become a statistic* of either market risk or inflation.

> **I can show you how to *make money without losing money*.**
> **It's simple. It is easy to understand.**
> **It's even easier to implement . . . if you have the right financial coach in your corner.**

Why remain vulnerable to an impoverished retirement? I'm about to show you how to make money with the money you have right now." This is the kind of money that will ***ensure your lifetime stream of income as you continue to build your financial nest-egg.***

CHAPTER THREE

Reward:
The 'Smart-Money' Pay-Off

A STABLE, ENJOYABLE RETIREMENT lifestyle should be your reward for a life of hard work. I'm talking about an easy-going, carefree retirement, not a post-career *nine-to-five* in a big-box retail warehouse. Those of you who know me have heard it before but I'll say it again:

Retirement should be all about play, not work!

Retirement is about something other than work. It's about living without having to worry about money. Not tomorrow, not in 10 years. *Real retirement* means never having to think about how much you have, how much you stand to lose, or having to worry about external forces maintaining control over the *destiny* of *your* retirement nest egg. In other words . . .

The reward of a 'real retirement' plan is less about how much money you have, more about how it helps you sleep at night.

In the last chapter, I talked about the longevity challenge. Here, I'm saying that you need to have **a retirement built to last**. You also need a plan made to keep pace with inflation and protect against risk. But let's face it, as we age, who wants a plan that requires constant attention? You may be a brilliant tactician when it comes to playing the market, but are you really winning the game if your tactics keep you strapped to a computer day and night – just to keep up with the latest trades? Of course not! How can a truly enjoyable, active retirement lifestyle maintain itself when it requires being in a constant state of vigil?

Forget about lugging a laptop up the trail to Machu Pichu . . . just to keep up with the market! You can't expect a reliable internet connection in Machu Pichu any more than you can expect income guarantees from Wall Street!

The Real 'Zen' of Retirement Maintenance

I can offer you a way to leave the laptop at home and truly enjoy the rest of your life. I can give you a guaranteed flow of lifetime income. This would be an income you cannot outlive. It requires no laptop vigil in the middle of the night. You would no longer need to be in constant contact with some broker posing critical decisions to be made on the fly – literally as you sit aboard an aircraft on your way to Peru. How ridiculous! How ludicrous!

I'm talking about the real *reward* of a life well-planned, a life without fear of inflation. I'm talking about taking morning walks on the beach without fear of market corrections. What if you no longer had to think about keeping your retirement portfolio up to speed? What if you knew you would always have adequate retirement income, no matter what happen to the rest of the planet?

What if you had the genuine reward of a safe, reliable plan designed to squeeze every last dime out of your hard-earned savings, ***while making the rest of your money grow at the same time?***

A Moment of Work to Ensure a Lifetime of Play

It takes some effort in the beginning, of course. We would sit down and map out the kind of practical day-to-day budget you would need to maintain a rewarding lifestyle. This would include everything from food and housing to health care and energy bills.

We would set aside needed cash in **liquid accounts** for emergencies. Other monies would go to vehicles that ensure against the need to liquidate any instrument in volatile markets. I'm not talking about money-market funds returning nothing but a place to park your assets. We would also need to plan for **long-term care**, the notorious culprit behind many a decimated nest-egg. Even sizeable estates can be destroyed by catastrophic illness.

To create a truly rewarding retirement lifestyle, we strip away any lingering worries over financial decimation due to that sudden medical emergency. More than 70 percent of Americans over 65 will be confronted by some type of health challenge, which could require some level of long-term care. It may surprise you but I have long-term care solutions that **avoid the astronomical costs of long-term-care insurance policies**, many of which have strict limits on benefit periods and payouts. I mean, why shell-out up to $2,000 a year ($2,500 or more annually for couples) on a long-term-care policy when you can build assets and provide for health care costs at the same time?

Multi-Tasking Annuities

If you have had the chance to read my other books, you know that I have been a long-time proponent of annuities. Some say I'm one of the foremost authorities on annuities in my industry. Over the many years I have helped virtually hundreds of people save their retirement lives through the use of annuities. These include new and innovative products that go far beyond the simple fixed annuity (which works very well for some people). A new generation of retirees, including many a former market investor, has discovered the power of modern annuities. The modern annuity may incorporate a seemingly infinite array of variations and features that can be layered to ensure all sorts of lifetime solutions for every kind of challenge.

In the aftermath of the Great Recession, as investors began to flock in droves toward asset protection, it has been my pleasure to watch the annuity gather the long-awaited recognition it truly deserves. Yet, as a life-long advocate of annuities, I also know that no two people would put an annuity to use in precisely the same way. As a nationally acclaimed annuity expert, I'm one of the few with extensive knowledge about how they work, how they can interact with other instruments, and how they can offset the risks of other investment strategies.

Risk Offset

Part of the "reward" I offer my clients is the ability to safeguard a lifetime income stream in such a way that it would offset risk of all kinds, from real estate holdings to mutual funds serving a higher-risk tolerance. But annuities offer much more than that. They can be structured in such a way as to create a kind of "longevity insurance." So there are all sorts of annuities, including "immediate annuities," which convert a lump sum into a lifetime income stream.

In every case, I can show you how to secure a rock-solid, lifetime flow of income, a **guaranteed source of income you cannot outlive, no matter how long you live.** In fact, you can structure different annuities with various "start" dates, each set to provide income at a chosen point in time. This method, in particular, can be a great way to set aside a growing asset for future income when you would need it most – after other instruments have run out of steam.

Reindel Strategies . . . Nationally Renowned

I have become widely known from coast to coast for providing all sorts of guaranteed, lifetime income for people in all walks of life. I have given a new outlook, the true "reward" of a carefree retirement lifestyle, to scientists, doctors, educators, and former Wall Street 'wolf' investors who jumped ship for the safe-harbor of annuities after the crash.

I have been able to rescue countless heart-broken retirees whose assets were decimated in one market crisis or another. And I'm not just talking about 2008. When you work with me you can forget about market "adjustments" and "corrections." I was there to pick up the pieces for many of my loyal clients after the tech crash, the 9/11 crash, the 2007 mortgage meltdown – you name it, I fixed it, and I did it with an array of streamlined tools to fit every lifestyle.

That's one of the many ways I remain above and separate from a vast majority of so-called "financial planners." Most have come over since the crash of 2008, after their brokerage houses and mutual fund sponsors took a deep dive and never resurfaced. Others have dealt with annuities, on the side, while being sidetracked by other types of instruments. *Few advisors have had the dedication to become a true expert in the vast annuity marketplace – I have!*

I have been able to salvage ravaged retirement portfolios to create not only an immediate, guaranteed stream of income, I've also been able to create additional income streams based on different products producing increased earnings and payouts. In other words, with these plans *the "reward" keeps on coming, like the 'Energizer' bunny*, for people who have let me help them achieve the lasting reward of carefree play, not work, during what should be the best years of your life.

The Conservative 'Safety' of Bonds and Other Myths

Before the dawning revolution of modern annuities, a so-called conservative bond investment program was considered the most reliable way to protect principal and generate earnings. We have since seen the truth about bonds. In extreme markets, like the one sparking the Great Recession, bonds reveal themselves to be what they are: securities. The bond market is part of the broader securities market. Bonds fail when, for example, municipalities default on the bonds they issue. In eras past, it would have been unthinkable for a city government to default on its bonds. But recently they have, and they will, and when they do, the bondholder will lose principal. Some bondholders have lost fortunes in principal.

I represent a class of retirement-safety tools that do not default on their promises. My products always deliver. I've never been one to brag or spew false promises about some golden goose with "unlimited potential." My promises come with the backing of A-plus Morningstar ratings and hundreds of grateful clients, all of whom would tell you this: You may think you're riding high on the risk-roller coaster until it drops into the valley of shadows, meaning overnight poverty after a market crash. My people will tell you how wonderful it is to be free of nightmares, free of anxiety, free to live their lives for the joy of the moment, each and every day on this marvelous terra firma.

To me, my clients define the true meaning of "reward." After all these years I've learned one thing: If you really get to know someone, he or she will tell you how important it is to simply live life every day without having to look over their shoulder in fear.

Long-term bond funds look great until interest rates begin to increase - because bond prices fall when rates rise. That's the way things are. You can "ladder" different types of bonds but they all eventually dance to the same drummer. And don't forget about inflation. You've probably heard about old-fashioned annuities lagging behind inflationary up-cycles. Well, times have changed, and annuities have changed. Anyone in my business will tell you that the modern version of this remarkable, flexible, undeniably dependable product *is not your grandfather's annuity.*

You can try to keep pace with inflation by investing in equities. This works very well during certain market cycles. Then it won't. You will find yourself scrambling to recapture what you lost and I have accurate, straightforward numbers to back up it up. The numbers clearly show the devastating, long-term effect of trying to keep pace with inflation through equities.

Real estate investments also may produce remarkable returns for a time, but we all know the ups and downs of real estate markets, which vary widely and unpredictably in different areas, based on jobs and other economic factors. For example, 'real estate investment trusts,' or REITS, allow real estate neophytes to invest in the industry, but great care must be taken when considering which markets a particular REIT might include. REITS crashed, by the way, to the point of near-extinction in the recent past of this nation although I'm happy to say that real estate markets are rising again, until they fall. All in a matter of time, right? As I said before: no need to panic, "it is what it is," as they say.

An Enduring Legacy of Strength and Reliability

All I'm saying is that my retirement solutions are a reward in themselves because they come fully backed by some of the most powerful institutions in the world. When multi-millionaire industrialists lost everything due to the market crash of 1929, only a wise and fortunate few were able to get crazy rich in the aftermath. Why? . . . *Because they had enough money in annuities* to not only live well, they had enough left over *to scoop up millions of dollars' worth of bargain stocks*, which turned to billions, which, in turn, created dynasties of wealth still flourishing today.

As I've been saying through the years, the humble "annuity" is still an unfolding story to be truly understood. Since the recent recession, I've been happy to see so many people wanting to hear me tell that story. Today, media that once tried to downplay the overwhelming value of a good annuity program now support this time-tested instrument. Yet, not all annuities are the same, nor do they work the same way for everyone. A recent Time magazine article noted that boomers now flock to the rewarding quality of so-called "longevity insurance" based on "immediate fixed annuities." Noting that such *annuities, in their traditional form, offer nominal earnings* and modest returns over a lifetime – in this case $6,950 annually on a $100,000 account - the story goes on to mention that "*a deferred immediate fixed annuity*" *can create nearly 10 times the return* (almost $64,000 a year) on the same investment.

This is one of a dozen reasons why you should have a deeply experienced annuity professional on your side when it comes to understanding the multitude of options in this often misunderstood realm of the financial services industry.

In It from the Beginning

I've been here all along. I didn't just "fall into" annuity sales after the 2009 market meltdown wiped out investor stock portfolios. I've been a believer in annuities from the very beginning, going back decades, in fact, and I can prove it. Later in this book I take pride in showing that, more than 15 years ago, I was widely supporting the invaluable, "safe-haven" power of annuities, concepts that were finally published nationwide in 2009 in the pages of my acclaimed book titled *Don't Die Broke* (Agate Publishers, 2009).

Long before that groundbreaking book came out, I sometimes felt like a voice in the wilderness, trying to get the word out about a safe, guaranteed method of protecting retirement assets *"no matter what"* happens on Wall Street. It wasn't easy. Like today, the stock market was roaring at the time. Mutual funds were fairly strong. Real estate values were rising through the proverbial roof. In that era, circa mid-2007, it was hard to convince an excitable crowd of naysayers to get off the Wall Street roller coaster and set aside assets for a guaranteed income they would never outlive. They just couldn't believe anything would happen to their soaring stocks, or their multiple 'buy-and-flip' real estate investments.

I was fortunately able to reach another kind of investor with the truth. They heard me speak at one or two of my seminars. They heard my message on the radio. They had the wisdom to understand that my words were potentially worth a pot of gold because they knew the basic physics of financial markets: *what goes up eventually comes down*. They worked with me to convert their hard-earned, at-risk retirement assets into guaranteed income for life.

Then the bottom fell out. October 2008 hit the vast majority of risk investors like a freight train. My clients were fine – in fact more than fine – as they told and re-told the story of how, and why, they were still living their retirement dreams as a mass of former retirees were heading back to work.

Retirement "Rewards" Defined . . .

Talk about *reward*! There is no better 'reward' at a time like that, the kind of moment in time destined to happen again. At that particular *time*, my clients came to realize that their serenity and peace-of-mind would never falter – that *their* tomorrow would be just another sunny day. Frightening headlines filled the dying newspapers. Dire news broadcasts poured out of every television set in America. TV news anchors announced that the stock market had been wiped out, that banks were gone, and that the real estate market was dead in its tracks.

I'll never forget the grateful phone calls I started getting from clients. But these were happy calls from people who had heard my voice and followed my advice. One long-time friend of mine said he had never realized how "rich" he really was until the great recession took hold of this country. His world would go on, unchanged - the ultimate reward. At the time, it was really rewarding for me to hear similar reactions from my other clients. Today, I know how well guaranteed-income planning can work for you. It truly is the most rewarding part of my job because I know, for a fact, that I've built a financial fortress for my clients. No matter what happens, their money will be protected against all odds.

If you decide to take my advice to heart and make a commitment to work with me, I am more than confident that I can do the same for you . . . I am *certain* of the outcome: My financial solutions will reward for years to come in your retirement, and that would be true for the legacy you choose to leave behind.

CHAPTER FOUR

Phoenix Rising:
Retirement Reborn

I WOULD LIKE TO introduce you to a man and his unexpectedly remarkable story. Here was a man who did everything right but wound up in the cold, without a retirement, not due to the recent recession but because of misguided advice that began decades before, when he faithfully started making contributions to a risk prone tradition.

This story is significant because it is not about the recent recession. In fact, this investor got through the recent crash and recession with little more than a 10% dent in his portfolio. He was one of the few.

*His particular financial debacle illustrates a more traditional timeline of market risk. His story is all about the devastating **loss of nearly 60% of his retirement savings during 20 long and equally destructive, years** before – and leading up to – 2008!*

I present this story to drive home the real point of this book: Catastrophic market loss is more than just a short-term phenomenon. It's part of life. It goes with the territory. Until now, we've largely covered more recent market losses that reduced millions of retirement portfolios by 50% or more, and this remains fresh in our collective memory. The irony is that, lately, not enough observers look back far enough – beyond the 10 to 13-year cycle previously discussed - to examine the actual, far-reaching, long-range effects of banking on a IRA based retirement strategies over 20 years or more. This story does just that, providing a glaringly clear snapshot of the much forgotten, multi-decade leading up to the more recent recession.

I think this story is especially important right now because you will undoubtedly hear some advisor insist that the recent catastrophe on Wall Street was only a "one-time thing." He may try to shrug it off as an economic "perfect-storm" that will "never happen again in our lifetime."

Maybe it won't. I hope it won't. But that's not the point of the upcoming story.

This story illustrates the manner in which an average, conservative market investor's path of financial destruction occurred slowly, but just as surely, and with even more devastating results over a period of time long-forgotten. His story is presented here, in his very own words, to provide living proof of the way markets beginning in the early 1980s left one of many people without a retirement plan.

For the sake of historic reference, back in the day - circa 1984 - it was said that making annual $2,000 contributions to an IRA would build the account to $1million by retirement age. Billions of investment dollars were based on this assumption. But few focus on the actual results of those lofty, market-based projections.

This story is an actual, numbers-based, clinical account of how such projections can, and will, fall short. Please note that this hard-working, average investor was careful. He was conservative. He trusted the conventional wisdom of the times from advisors and personal financial publications. Instead, he lost money, continually, steadily, traumatically . . .

This process kept on until he finally walked into my office after the last recession and said, "I've had enough." I'm happy to say that this is not only a true story, it also has a happy ending, by the way, and with much food for thought in the interim.

I would now like to introduce you to one of my more recent clients. His name is Carl.

D.R.

Carl's Story

"Thanks for the introduction, Dave.

"And for everyone reading this factual, real-life account, I want to assure you that Dave's words are true. Not long ago, after surfing the channels, I stumbled onto one of Dave's Sunday morning radio shows and unlike other shows of a similar nature, I began listening to what this man had to say. I was at the point that I needed someone with a different orientation help me plan for retirement.

"The more I listened, the more interested I got. Finally, I found myself listening to him every Sunday for a month or two before I finally said, "I've got to call this guy." I didn't really have a solid plan for retirement at the time. At my age at the time, I should have had something in place years before. But for all those many years, I thought I *was* doing something - something that would leave me in good shape in the end. Then I finally realized – after so many ups and downs in the stock market - that I was getting nowhere fast. I had been investing in stocks.

As everybody knows, 2008 came along and everything smacked into a stone wall, financially. But my story goes farther back, and by then, I really didn't know what else to do. By 2008, I'd already held very little esteem for stock brokers. I'd been through quite a few and found that none of them really knew how to set me up in retirement. As a matter of fact, to this day I don't know if any of them really cared about me or not. I'll explain, but let's begin at the beginning.

As we move along in life we begin to realize that a broker is really interested in two things: buying stock and selling stock for commissions. Beyond that, I got a feeling that most of these guys really don't know what's going on - not with any particular stock they might try to sell you. It's as if they're trying to find a crystal ball, and I knew there was something else I was supposed to do. I just didn't know what, and I didn't know where to go. I didn't know that people like David Reindel were even out there – someone who could actually pick up the pieces and point me in the right direction.

History Speaks

Unfortunately, my story is fairly typical and more common than not. I first entered the stock market around 1985, when I was in my early 40s. Back then, banks were paying 10% and 12% interest a year! That's what I had actually been earning in bank accounts and money markets, which is hard to believe today, but there we were. It didn't take much to save and plan for retirement. All you had to do was work hard and count on the strength and dependability of the American economy - also the way we did business back then, which has changed.

With basic savings accounts and a little discipline, I finally had $10,000 to invest. Oh, how we took everything for granted back then! Everybody had a pocketful of money. I mean, money was no object in the Reagan years. I think back to his administration and the fond memory of the stable economy we once had. It was unbelievable: 10% interest . . . from a bank CD! Today you get 1% percent or less from some of the same banks we had to bail out after '08 . . . I mean, where did the bailout money go? Never mind.

Conventional Wisdom

Back in the beginning, when I had my first $10,000 in savings, I never questioned the conventional wisdom at the time. Somebody told me that if I put $2,000 a year into my IRA I'd have a million dollars by the time I wanted to retire. That sounded great to me and I was a believer. There were no real financial train wrecks back then, only short-term adjustments from time to time. Things kept growing, so I started putting $2,000 a year into the IRA, which was the maximum allowed by the IRS at the time.

After that, through a broker I bought into a mutual fund with another $10,000. I stayed with the broker for several years, buying stock here and there, maybe 100 shares of, say, Kodak, then something else. I thought we'd do pretty well. In fact, back then I thought I was going to make a pile of money. We went into Kodak, Rubbermaid and Pfizer – good companies at the time - but not really big names, although Pfizer was considered a hot stock at that time, so I initially bought 100 shares of Pfizer, then I bought another 100 shares after that, then the stock doubled. That's how things were in those days. By the mid-1990s – after transferring years of contributions from my IRA to stocks – I had around $100,000 with the broker. Not bad.

Warning Signs

Then things began to sour, and I hope young people learn from what I'm about to pass along: At the end of the year I called up my broker to wish him a happy holiday season. Instead of just wishing me the same, he nearly jumped down my throat, saying, "You've got to get into a couple of hot new stocks. If you want to retire early you gotta' do this, gotta' do this, gotta' do this."

I was sitting there, stunned, thinking this guy knew something I didn't. He wanted me to transfer cash, and some of my Pfizer stock, and other assets into these "hot new" stocks. He kept saying, *"You gotta' do it, gotta' do it."* I trusted the guy . . . so I went ahead and did it. We moved $50,000 into his "hot new stocks." We were into the late 1990s by then and, little did I know, we were on the brink of a major crash on the S&P.

This is something younger investors really need to hear: The crash of '08 has not been the only gut-wrenching drop on the DOW and S&P. In my lifetime, we have seen many, many gut-wrenching drops on the DOW and S&P. Please, remember that!

The late-1990s S&P crash took away my $50,000. But this was only the beginning. From 2000 all the way through the wipe-out in October, 2008, we had *many more* upsets in stock and bond markets. Older guys like me remember this, but I'm afraid a lot of us will soon forget.

As soon as the market begins to top out – like it seems to be doing right now - down you go! The market could be ready to slip *back in the tank anytime.*

Anyway, after putting my $50,000 in that so-called "red-hot" tech stock, within days we watched a 'mystery bubble' in technology burst like a balloon in a lightning storm. Turns out, a lot of those stocks were based on air and a promise, and I was alone at that point, trying to track my "hot" stocks as they went down, down and down. This was so depressing I stopped watching them altogether, thinking they would eventually bounce back . . . big mistake.

In a heartbeat, my red-hot tech stocks went from somewhere in the $30s down to $2 a share, almost nothing.

I hope what I'm about to say won't turn prophetic – especially with the market as it is today – but here's the moral of the story about "buy and hold:" I did "hold" on to those tech stocks, right down to the bitter end . . . and they never came back. This is the reality brokers and stock-pumping publications never seem to address: *You can lose it all. I did.* My $50,000 was **gone**. Half of everything I'd ever had was wiped out.

I tried to call my broker. Lo and behold, I couldn't get hold of him. Right then, I began to ask myself if this guy ever really knew what was going on. And if he did, why didn't he call me before the shares really took a dive? I didn't know it at the time, but that's not the way it works. *You* buy. *They* make money. From there, you're really on your own.

Unless you're dealing with a rock-solid product like a good annuity, how can a stock broker maintain hundreds of client stock portfolios at the same time and keep an eye on every one of them? Here's the truth: no need to be a math genius, *they can't.* Maybe I should have been watching more closely myself, but for what? I thought I could count on my broker. I know better now. I pulled out all of my money and closed the account. Now, I can clearly hear the way he sounded when he pushed those stocks. Back then I thought I was getting an inside tip, just for me, but it was pure hype. He'd been humping the same stuff on the phone to everybody else, obviously out to boost his year-end commissions, at the expense of his clients.

Do you think that kind of mentality is still around today? Don't kid yourself: of course it is!

I went on to another brokerage and experienced the same treatment. They were selling stocks, buying stocks, and I didn't seem to be part of the action. Is there a pattern here? There is: These people really don't know what they're doing. They're selling a product, they're buying a product, they're making commissions. That's all. It became apparent to me, kind of late in the game, that I was going nowhere fast. I saw my totals go down again, then up just enough to keep me in stocks. Then they were off again. I felt the way you feel after playing slot machines. The system feeds out a few little jackpots, but you walk out of the casino empty-handed in the end. I said to myself, "This is not what I need."

Forget the bygone S&P dive, the tech-stock crash and the post-9/11 dump . . . ouch, that one really hurt. By then, a lot of us wanted out, but we let things ride because we didn't know where else to go. Sticking with the old "buy and hold" concept, I let it ride like everybody else. I kept adding to my savings, really trying to recover, hoping the market would keep growing. By 2005, I had accumulated somewhere around 200,000, which sounded pretty good, but I knew - after all those years - that I should have had much more. So, I bought more mutual funds and some E-bond savings bonds.

The Final Outcome

I gave my SEP, IRA and my existing brokerage account to a local broker who put it all into mutual funds and they did alright, moving up to $250,000. But the year was 2006 and that was the sum total of gains I'd made *since 1992.*

The funds took another hit during the crash of 2008, but I was lucky this time; the management team was highly skilled. I lost maybe 10 percent through the crash. Not much. Luckily, I had other investments in addition to the $250,000 but, all together, *they weren't worth much more than $400,000 . . . after more than 20 years in the market!*

At that point, I stepped back and thought, "What now?" Do I stay in the market? Do I gamble on the chance that it won't happen again? Or do I look at my age? Do I face the facts, cut my losses, and find a plan that won't let me down?

The Reindel Solution

I decided that I wanted to be able to *actually retire.* So, I went with David Reindel.

I didn't want to risk yet another *slump* in the economy, nor do I want to take that risk today. By the time I got to David, I had only $440,000 *after investing for more than 25 years.* So much for the promise of $1 million they said I'd have if I "stayed the course." I'd heard enough. It was time to get off the roller coaster.

David put my savings into three different annuity contracts, each offering an incentive bonus. They're all fixed indexed annuities and the bonuses can be used to offset fees – in case I need to make early withdrawals over the amount allowed by the contract every year . . . so don't listen to everything you hear about annuity fees. When I bought my annuities, the plan was to wait at least five years before taking payments, so it's not like a 20-year stretch and I'll be getting those payments soon.

I told David I'd be willing to live on $50,000 to $60,000 a year when all is said and done, being single and without significant expenses. In a couple of years, I'll be able to draw enough income out of my contracts and use that money - in addition to Social Security - to get where I need to be. (Social Security planning is another important part of the picture . . . something people tend to take for granted, but that's another story.)

When Dave was done, I was set for life. Now I know my money won't vanish overnight in some stock market crash. If the market goes up, my annuity earnings go up. If the market goes down, I won't lose my gains. Mainly, I'll never lose a penny of the original principal I put into my annuities. That's what matters. I now look forward to a nice income I can count on and that's good enough for me. I'm not looking to own four houses with four Bentleys in each garage. That's not me. I'm more interested in peace of mind.

A Treasure in Trust

I asked David if I could put more money into the annuities. If he'd been like some of the brokers I've known, he would have been all too happy to sell me more annuities. But he said, "No, I'd rather see you build up your cash and let the annuities do their thing." I was impressed. *I've never had anybody in the financial world give me an answer like that.* David is always very honest, which is one of many reasons I trust him so much. After talking to him, getting to know him, after listening to his show, I know he'll give me straight answers. If I was talking to a stock broker, the answer would always be the same: "buy more stock."

I feel very certain that the only place a retirement can be safe is with David Reindel's kind of program. I've also heard that you can get into the wrong kind of annuity, so you need a real expert. This is Dave's passion. Annuities are all he does. I've since learned that he knows more about annuities than anybody in the business. In other words, this man gives me confidence - which is something I hadn't had in years before I met him.

Now I know where I'll be financially in five years, and when you know where you're going, you can begin to adjust to the kind of lifestyle you'll be able to depend on. This, to me, is *a real treasure*. This is worth far more than pinning your hopes on a spinning a roulette wheel in some casino. This is a given. This should be elementary logic when you're ready to retire.

After the last crash, people are really fed up with the hype and ridiculous fees of traditional brokers, and I do think more and more people are going into annuities. I also think annuity carriers are going to get a lot more competitive and innovative to meet the demand.

True Colors

I can't finish the story without sharing my stranger-than-fiction finale: When I told my last broker I was getting out, they gathered around and sternly warned me about "playing around with my money." They said I needed to keep my money in stock.

Then they kept pressing me to tell them what I was going to do. Finally, I gave in and said I was going into annuities. You should have seen the change. They said "Annuities?! What?! Are you sure that's what you want to do?" They talked about the so-called "high fees." They said I was making a mistake. They did everything they could to keep my money.

I say this because when you decide to get out of the casino, this is what you can expect to hear. I stood my ground. I said I'd been talking to David Reindel who had explained things to me like no one ever had. I said, "This guy really knows his stuff," and I was right. Everything turned out the way Dave said it would.

But you may have to hang tough when you're ready to bail because things might get nasty. Here's how it played out at the bitter end: My soon-to-be ex-broker asked me for a last chance. She said she had some annuities to sell me but wanted to talk to her head-of-sales, her supervisor, because she probably didn't know much about annuities in the first place. I gave her a chance.

What happened next still lingers in my memory.

After getting hold of her supervisor, she said that when she merely brought up the word "annuities," he threw up his arms, walked off and shouted, "Who understands annuities?" Desperate, my broker changed tactics, going on about fees and things in a last ditch to keep my business. But I already knew all about "fees," especially the endless nickel-and-dime fees and penalties associated with mutual funds. "And what happens to market gains," I said, "when you get hit with horrendous losses, which are going to keep happening again and again?"

When I said that, she finally turned into someone who seemed to be in cahoots with the devil. The difference was day and night, not unlike the bedroom scene in *The Exorcist*. I could hardly believe I was talking to the same person. In other words, she was awfully nasty in the end. After all those years, I had finally learned that many of these people are not only poorly informed - they really ***are not*** working in your best interest.

This would be my last and final brokerage firm.

Smooth Sailing

There will never be horrendous losses with Dave's annuities. Instead, I get 7% percent when the market is up. I lose nothing when the market is down. They even add a bonus to offset a 5% fee when you're ready to come out of the annuity and take distributions. Add in all the gains and other company contributions and what you get in the end is way more than 5% when you draw the money out. And when it comes to risk, I've been there.

The Dow is up and over 18,000 and we're still threatened by trouble overseas. Anything can trigger a drop on the S&P, like . . . gee, I forget. Never mind. Who wants to remember? I don't have to anymore.

I still remember a quote by Ronald Reagan when he predicted what might happen to the future of our economy and American retirees. Reagan said something about "freedom being very fragile" and that "we might be one generation away from losing it." It seemed like a cryptic remark at the time, but what he said rings hauntingly true today.

I think we see now what had been in the works long ago. Now we need to prepare.

CHAPTER FIVE

Retirement Pillars and Foundations Lifetime Income

I'M GOING TO show you how to make the most of what will be one of the most reliable sources of your retirement income. For decades, the ins-and-outs of this critically important treasure chest were misunderstood, so people often ignored the wealth it can provide when developed to its full potential. Retirees would simply throw that potential away, essentially grabbing the low-hanging portion of its fruits, unaware that they had lost a major helping of what they could have enjoyed . . . *for the rest of their lives.*

Unfortunately, you won't find much information about this kind of lucrative potential at the source. The treasure custodians are very helpful when it comes to application, but they are limited in the amount of advice they can provide. To be fair, it would take too much time away from other applicants waiting in line, and employment guidelines discourage them from stepping into the role of quasi-financial advisors, which could cause problems. It isn't part of their job description. Therefore, please don't blame government workers for an inability to lay it all out. It is YOUR job to investigate your options.

I am about to make that investigative process smooth and easy to understand. Truth be known, if every incoming retiree knew the facts about this marvelous treasure chest, it would cost Uncle Sam a lot more money. So, at a time when the feds are trying to cut back on entitlement programs, they tend to leave it up to us to work things out. Again, don't blame Uncle Sam.

Advisors with 'Other' Priorities

Unfortunately, most private-sector financial advisors avoid discussion of tapping the full potential of your treasure-chest, hoping to divert your attention to commission-rich products of every stripe. Let's face it, there's nothing 'in it' for the advisor when it comes to tapping into your government money. In their own best interest, most of them devote *their* time toward earning commissions when they meet with you. Some are trained to do this. Some of them are even required to do this by their employers.

I am independent and quite different, as you have probably begun to see. Other planners with my outlook are out there, too, but are few and far between. The way we see it, a happy client is going to continue to be a loyal client. This is one of many reasons why we make sure to maximize every possible avenue of retirement income for our people. Frankly, this makes good, business sense, to my way of thinking. I also really, truly love helping people, as you probably noticed at the beginning of the book.

You also discovered, in the last chapter, that not all advisors think like I do – they're out for themselves, not your best interest. In fact, many people are *still* unaware of independent retirement *advocates*, people like me. Congratulations: *you* are!

I've devoted a significant portion of this book to the maximization of benefits solely devoted to *you*, not me. Later, of course, we'll take a look at a combination of elements in order to create your ultimate retirement solution. But, as the saying goes: "first-things-first."

The Perfect Safety Net to Catch a Golden Goose

Let's cut to the chase: I've been referring to Social Security, of course, since the beginning of this chapter. Most of us have made steady contributions to our future Social Security benefits for the better part of our lives. For most people, a big chunk of annual federal taxes go to Social Security, which may be available at 62 . . . but WAIT! Stop right there.

If you know anything about me, you know how I feel about taking benefits at 62. As I see it, taking "early" benefits at any time before your Full Retirement Age is akin to shooting yourself in the financial foot. That's right. Most boomers will reach their Full Retirement Age at 66. For others their FRA is either sooner or later than that but the message is clear: Take early benefits and you lose . . . BIG TIME. I want you to hold off on taking benefits until, at the very least, you reach your Full Retirement Age (see *www.ssa.gov* to determine your FRA).

But we're not done yet, not by a long shot! *Most people really need to wait until age 70* to tap into their Social Security benefit. I'll show you some numbers in upcoming pages that you may find rather astounding. By then you will see why you stand to kill the one "Golden Goose" most people have for retirement, and when you kill the goose . . . there go the golden eggs.

Wait until just the right moment and you will grow your Social Security benefit by more than 50%, as compared to dipping into your benefit early-on. Yes, *you could lose nearly 50% of your benefit.*

This is one of the least understood, most important secrets in the entire Social Security program. All you have to do is wait while your money compounds, and it will, risk-free. Again, this kind of growth is almost unheard of among fixed-income products and it means that at age 70 you will receive a fully compounded benefit . . . *guaranteed for life.*

But we're far from done. I have many more variations, rules, techniques in mind that will help you maximize your Social Security benefit even further . . . much further. I'll show you how to maximize benefits for a loved one after you have passed on because Social Security is designed to work in several important, beneficial ways, which will open the door to the full potential of this often misunderstood financial instrument. As you will discover in upcoming chapters, you can suspend the flow of monthly checks until a later time, which could greatly increase your monthly benefit check for the rest of your life.

Again, you might not spot this important factor, at first glance, as you browse the Social Security Administration web site, and don't expect Social Security Administration employees to help you in this area for the reason stated above. It's not their job. This is where *you* come in, and I'm here to help!

We Know the Ropes

I can't say it enough: Before you hit the "go" button with Social Security, you need to wade in and do your homework. You'll get a lot of help in the next few chapters but you should make an appointment with someone like me. The SSA system is fraught with tricky little twists and turns. We've been there, countless times. We know the ropes and can help guide you through the Social Security process.

Even more important, I can help you put the right things in place *before* you make the kinds of mistakes that equate to retirement income set-backs for retirees . . . *for the rest of their lives*. I can create a highly customized plan to wrap around your Social Security income, a plan geared specifically to you and your situation. As I've said, I'm different than other advisors. I take all the time necessary, with each of my clients, to make sure your *entire-lifetime* plan will work properly for you.

When it comes to maximizing your future monthly income from Social Security, the difference between planning a few advance moves – or not - could put *hundreds of thousands* of extra dollars in your pocket, extra money that would allow for extra travel, nicer hotels and restaurants, the ability to give nicer gifts to your grandchildren.

Unfortunately, too many people take that impulsive leap and grab at the "low-hanging" fruit of the Social Security system. By then, it's too late. I know I've said it twice, but it frustrates me to watch people make the early grab, just because they can. Way too many times, people come into my office after-the-fact, thinking they can somehow reverse the process. Well, you can't. *However*, if you are one of these people, no worries: I have many other solutions that can make a major difference in your retirement lifestyle.

You Are Absolutely "Entitled"

One reason for my frustration is that I know, for a fact, that you are *absolutely entitled* to the maximum potential of your Social Security income. You paid for it! If you are over 55 and reading this book in the Year 2015, you should expect it. After all, you and millions of other Americans have been paying into the Social Security system for your entire working lives. After watching people struggle through the horrors of the Great Depression, President Franklin D. Roosevelt established Social Security, back in 1935, to see to it that every working American would have something to live on during our golden years.

Not the Be-All . . .

Keep in mind that Social Security was never intended to provide all income needs in retirement. It was put in place to keep us out of the soup lines of some future "great depression" (recession, whatever). It was, and still is, a good system, however abused by certain individuals. It is one of the few government entitlement programs that still works, and it would work just as well as originally intended, if politicians do the right thing.

Why do we see routine headlines describing projected problems with Social Security? Problems grew as politicians discovered mountains of cash in the Social Security trust fund. They saw the money as overgrown "surplus" that would not be used for years, so they "borrowed" from the fund to benefit their political constituents - even though the money had been carefully earmarked for future retirees, including the Generation Xrs and Millennials defining today's younger investor.

This is at the fundamental root of "problems" with our Social Security trust fund. The only real "problem" is that the *borrowers* somehow forgot to put the money back in the fund before some left Congress. Others are still there, on Capitol Hill. Meanwhile, a growing heap of I.O.U.s is sitting in the fund, and there it will remain until the IOUs become a political issue for taxpayers.

Risk vs. Guaranteed Safety

The following numbers illustrate what can happen to the same account heading in different directions. One route would follow S&P index activity from January 1, 2000, through January 1, 2012, with each example showing an initial $100,000 premium, and without withdrawals affecting the account. Market value is based on historic activity on the S&P during the period, not that the S&P would react the same way in the future. Nor would it represent the future activity of an index annuity.

Here, we simply assume a hypothetical index annuity with a 5% crediting method based on a point-to-point cap and reset. It also shows hypothetical results from having an Income Rider with a 6.5% annual rate of return for income purposes – again, I'm just giving you a glimpse of the past and how the index annuity performed at one point in time versus assets at risk in the market.

With assets left to ride the S&P 500 Index from age 70 forward, we began with $100,000 in the Year 2000, adding in the factor of a 5.5% average return through the period. After taking a beating from both the tech-crash in 2000 and again during the 9/11 market panic in 2001, by the Year 2002, our 70-year-old's account is down to $59,882. It begins to struggle out of the soup, as many investors well recall, recovering back to $99,939 by 2007 - still a few bucks short of where it began in 2000, but our 70-year-old market player has nearly recovered his money . . . but only after *seven long years*! Then, the account tanks again, in 2008, dropping back to $61,477.

Heartbreak Hill on the S&P

Is this heartbreaking? That's the problem with mathematical charts and graphs: they cannot convey emotions. How would you have felt at that point? After eight, long years, your once-upon-a-time $100,000 nest egg is worth roughly what it was worth after the tech and 9/11 "corrections" at the beginning of the decade.

Finally . . . and I mean *finally* . . . by January 1, 2012, your account has almost recovered, nearing the break-even point, or $97,069. It would hypothetically move on to a value of $125,801 sometime in the latter part of 2013 . . . finally. . . . Impressive, huh? . . . *Not!*

Now let's look at our Index Annuity account during the same time period. Impervious to the ravages of the market, after the tech crash of 2000, and the 9/11 market panic, by 2002 our $100,000 account is now worth $120,795 (at the same time the market account is down to $59,882). By 2007, after increasing steadily at a compounding rate of 5.5%, our Index Annuity model is now worth $165,000 (as the market account struggles back to its zero-gains-starting- value of $99,939).

Again immune to market mayhem during the 2008 crash, the Index Annuity account is worth $176,257 (as the S&P account dives again to $61,477). At the same end-point on January 1, 2012, the Index Annuity account is valued at $226,749 . . . *while the market account struggles back to zero-break even at $97,069*! At some point in the future, into 2013, the Index Annuity has reached a value of $241,487. The market account has "bounced back" to a mere $125,801 . . . "stumbled back" is the better way to put it.

I'm not saying that the market will collapse so many times - like it did in the above illustration - over the next 12-year to 13-year period. But who can say? In prior chapters, I think we've presented a host of factors indicating that it very well *might*. For now, you can see the difference in results in the end-game scenario: ***Your money would have been worth $241,487 in the Index Annuity while the S&P market account would have been valued at a paltry $125,801.***

Isn't it about time to consider some kind of 'financial insurance' for your retirement?

Before moving on, let's put the scenario above into real-money numbers, on the ground, in a hypothetical retirement: At age 70, the S&P account would have provided $3,294 in income. At age 70, the

Index Annuity would have provided $6,644 in income – more than $3,300 in income!

Now imagine putting $100,000 into an Index Annuity at age 60 and let it grow without taking withdrawals until age 70. Assuming the same 5.5% compounding return over the 10-year period, your account would provide $13,282 of income per year from an account worth $241,487. Your friend, stuck in the S&P, would see about half that amount in annual income.

Knowing back then what you know right now, what investment model might you have chosen to fill your Income Gap? Need I ask?

Tip: How to Narrow the SS Income Gap

Alright, we touched on 'spousal planning' for Social Security benefits in a previous chapter. Now I'm going to go deep and show you how to really work the system for the best possible results. When some people read this, they may be a bit dismayed if they're already filed and set their benefits at lesser amounts for life.

If not, how would you like to make sure your spouse receives the MAXIMUM Social Security income? Would both spouses be able to file early and increase their benefit at the same time? Here's how to put the Social Security "Spousal Benefit" option to work for you:

Spousal Benefit in Motion

Let's look at a monstrously charming couple named Herman and Lily and see how they were able to increase their total, lifetime Social Security benefit by several hundred thousand dollars.

Let's assume that they want to file early, at age 62. Let's also assume that after a lifetime of taxed earnings they would be eligible for a total (combined) lifetime Social Security benefit of $583,000. We talked about the consequences of early filing, and yet, maybe your situation calls for just that – as in the case with Lily and Herman. Based on their life expectancy, they would earn $583,000 if they did nothing other than file at 62. Here's something else that may surprise you: If they both trigger the "Spousal Planning Option" offered through the Social Security, based on the same life expectancy in this model, they would receive $898,000! That's right: They would increase their total, combined, lifetime benefit by $315,000!

How so? Come in and let us analyze your situation. I'll show you how to use different illustrations using available Social Security planning options. I've given you a taste of this one, quick example just to show what lies hidden in some of the lesser-known provisions of the Social Security rule book. It is obviously WELL WORTH exploring. Wouldn't you agree? My analysis will give you the highest possible level of family benefits, and our experience can help put it all together.

Herm and Lil Decide to File and Suspend

Let's first look at how File and Suspend can work using a typical method.

First, Herman's Primary Income Amount at age 66 would be $2,336. This is what he would receive at Full Retirement Age. But rather than receive his benefits right away, he decides to File and Suspend.

At the same time, Lily reaches her FRA. Instead of taking the usual route to start receiving her own monthly check, she instead decides to file for Spousal **Benefits.**

Let's try that again: HE decides to File and *Suspend* – SHE files for Spousal benefits. Having filed for Spousal Benefits – meaning she now gets 50% of Herman's Social Security Benefits – let's say her monthly benefit check (her PIA) is $1,062 . . . again, after filing for Spousal Benefits.

Here's an interesting twist to the tale: because she is taking half of Herman's benefit, or $1,062, *her* benefit will keep growing at the rate of 8% per year until she turns 70. Stay with me here because this is part of an amazing array of options in the system: Because Herman opted to File and Suspend, HIS untouched benefit has been growing all along. At age 70, Herman now begins to receive his benefit, which has grown from $2,336 up to $3,030. Herman will get $3,030 per month for the rest of his life.

Now it's Lily's turn. When she reaches age 70, she files for her own benefits – recall that she had only filed for her "Spousal" Benefit, back when she reached her FRA at age 66. Now, at age 70, because she delayed taking her own benefit, she will get $1,488 per month for the rest of her life – up from the $1,062 she would have received, had she decided to start taking her own benefit at Full Retirement Age.

In other words, together, they will now receive $4,518 per month, instead of the $3,398 monthly benefit they would have received, had they gone the conventional route most people take upon reaching Full Retirement Age, when most people just file for their own benefits. Little do they know what can happen when you know how to take advantage of every option made available by the Social Security Administration.

For Herm and Lil, the difference is more than $1,000 a month!

Ralph and Alice demonstrate the "Restricted Application" Strategy

Here's where Ralph decides to get off the bus for good and retire at 66. Both he and Alice have reached 66, their Full Retirement Age. Both now qualify for $1,000 each in Social Security benefits every month.

But here's yet another twist: Upon retirement, Alice files and decides to collect her $1,000 monthly benefit check. At the same time, Ralph has heard of another option. Instead of filing in the conventional manner, Ralph decides to file what is known as a *"Restricted Application."*

Having filed a Restricted Application, Ralph can now collect his "Spousal Benefit" of $650 – or 50% of Alice's PIA benefit – and let his own Primary Income Amount continue to grow until his 70th birthday. These are called "Delayed Retirement Credits" in Social Security vernacular, by the way: When you 'delay' taking benefits, you increase your 'delayed retirement credits,' growing your benefit by 8% per year, *for four full years*, thus increasing your benefit *by 32%* at age 70!

At age 70, Ralph's benefit is now $1,320 a month. Added to Alice's $1,000 benefit, their combined $2,320 goes a lot further. The Restricted Application Strategy was designed to maximize Social Security and Survivor Benefits for people who have reached their Full Retirement Age. Simply put, one spouse goes for the standard benefits; the other spouse files a Restricted Application to receive a half benefit while earning Delayed Retirement Credits.

Do the 'Switch' - Coordinate Spousal Benefits

For many couples today, these little strategies mount up to a BIG difference in lifetime income. All told, when referring to the planning options described above, we call them "Switch Strategies." As you look at essentially limited benefits in the beginning, you have the ability to "switch" to much larger benefits later on.

This is so important, I like to put the spotlight on the essentials to make sure your Social Security options remain firmly in mind. In summary: Once you reach your Full Retirement Age, your FRA, you then have two primary methods available to significantly increasing your family benefits . . . for the rest of your life. These methods are:

- The **Restricted Application Strategy**

- The **File and Suspend Strategy**

But wait! What about taxation? Don't they tax our Social Security benefits these days? They do, and how! Here again, I have a few little-known secrets to minimize taxation of your Social Security benefits as well.

Social Security Taxation Strategies

This area of Social Security benefits planning still falls under the general category of Spousal Planning. But first let me say that I can't pack every tiny detail into this book or your eyes would quickly glaze over and my message would be lost in the minutiae.

I hope to have a chance to meet you in person, to get all the details necessary from you, and to allow us to step in and help you from behind the scenes with your application process. If you go no further with this book and would like some help in this area, please call me at 800.639.5113 or find more contact information through my web site at *www.DavidReindel.com*.

Minimizing S.S. Taxation

Moving on, for this 'bewitching' illustration let's look at a single woman in retirement. We'll call her "Endora" and take a quick look at both the "before" and "after" of her income and the taxation of her income: Her Social Security benefit is $10,000 a year. She receives additional income from a pension to the tune of $18,000 a year. Neither of these numbers will change in either the "before" or "after" in this illustration.

What WILL change, however, is her taxable interest. Without doing anything, Endora's taxable interest is $20,000. Left unattended, she would have to write a check to Uncle Sam in the amount of $5,536 this year, in order to pay income taxes on her Social Security and pension benefits.

I have an easy method at my fingertips that would reduce her annual tax bill from $5,536 DOWN to only $801. Yes, you're looking at the right numbers! With one simple move I can reposition her interest. Instead, her formerly taxable interest would become "deferred interest." When this happens, Endora will save $4,735 on her annual tax bill. Wow! All she needs is the right guidance in order to reposition her money. In this situation, I have a certain type of annuity in mind.

I had to look twice when I first discovered this simple but critical tax-savings device. It was that good, and right there all along! How had Endora's Social Security become taxable? Given the amount of her total annual income, they would probably base her tax bill on half her Social Security benefit, also all of her $18,000 annual pension income and $20,000 taxable interest, which becomes $43,000 in Adjusted Gross Income for the year.

Over $25,000: Reduce Your Social Security Tax

If you earn more than $25,000 and currently wonder how to reduce your Social Security tax bill, I have a couple of pointers.

Remember, Endora's actual *total* income was $48,000, by the way, before being adjusted down to $43,000. Most people have no clue that the IRS provides retirees with **an exception** to the overall taxation rule when it comes **to the calculation of your tax bill**.

This comes in the form of a break *for monies within annuities* – I'm talking about interest earned inside the annuity, or your *earned* annuity-interest. You should know that *deferred annuity interest* is not included in your tax equation for the actual year in which it was earned. When you have earnings from, say, your indexed annuity in a given year, you would not pay tax on the earnings in the year they were earned – you pay tax on those earnings when they are finally *withdrawn* from your account.

Handled correctly, this can create a very positive outcome for your retirement lifestyle. Your **annuity earnings would be allowed to compound and grow** exponentially. Your eventual withdrawals could be made at such a time when your principal had been allowed to increase, thus providing extra value in the account to help offset the tax bill. In other words, if you took a distribution today and paid the entire tax bill, it would take a sizeable chunk out of your retirement portfolio. Tax-deferred earnings create more money to foot the tax bill in the future, as you make withdrawals from the account.

Back to our $25,000 Social Security Taxation threshold: If Endora earns more than $25,000 she could take advantage of the tax shelter, utilizing the IRS exception for earned annuity interest. Again, taxation on deferred annuity interest is deferred until the year she would begin making withdrawals from her annuity.

This came about after Congress realized the potential hardship for retirees when – most likely – our Congressional leaders were in the act of (again) raising taxes on Social Security benefits, which, in fact, were never meant to be taxed when FDR fostered the program back in the 1930s. Whenever Congress dips into Social Security money through taxation, or otherwise, they sometimes give us something to ease the bite . . . which is precisely why these methods and exclusions are available to YOU. All you have to do is to *take advantage of everything you have coming*, because *it's all there for a reason.*

Annuity Planning Endorsed by U.S. Presidents

Whether your looking at Social Security taxation or guaranteed income strategies, or both, the use of annuities for retirement planning has been endorsed by two U.S. presidents for a reason! Presidents Bush and Obama issued resolutions during their administrations, noting the importance of annuities as a way to reduce – or even eliminate – risk for our retirement savings.

Annuities have been designed to participate in an ever-increasing share of insurance company investments in the market . . . while protecting both *your earnings* and *your principal* from risk!

Why not take advantage of this incredible instrument? The Fixed Index Annuity and other types of annuities have not only been endorsed by the government, they have been given unique tax advantages under IRS rules. How many other types of investments can make that claim?

Will My Benefit Be Taxed?

To determine your "Threshold Income" simply add up the following: Half your Social Security Income, plus ALL of your other income including:

- **Wages and Pensions**

- **Dividends and Capital Gains**

- **Business Income**

- *Tax-Exempt Interest* **on things like savings bonds and municipal bonds**

I can hear you ask, "Do you mean *tax exempt* bond interest is counted? I thought it was tax exempt!"

It was exempt in another part of the financial equation. But when it comes to your Social Security benefit, it is counted as Threshold Income. Surprise. Only when you have ongoing compounding interest in another kind of instrument would your earnings be exempt.

Income Thresholds work like this:

Singles and Social Security Taxes

- Single taxpayers earning *$34,000 and up will have 85%* of their Social Security benefits taxed as income.

- Singles earning between *$25,000 and $34,000 a year will have 50%* of their Social Security money taxed.

- Only when a single person earns *less than $25,000 a year* would his or her Social Security money be *tax-free*.

Married Couples and Social Security Taxes

- Married couples *earning less than $32,000* would see *no Social Security benefit taxation.*

- Otherwise, couples earning *$32,000 to $44,000 would be taxed on 50%* of their benefits.

- Couples earning *more than $44,000 a year would be taxed on 85%* of their benefits.

SSA Tax Planning Important for Retirees

Social Security taxation can be a serious matter for people living on fixed incomes in retirement. Planning for taxation of your benefits becomes a must-do for most people, and can be as important as any other form of benefits planning. It's all part of the overall strategy to maximize your benefits, using everything the federal government intended for you to use, in order to strengthen your retirement lifestyle (and stay off welfare).

First, you need to come in and let us evaluate the potential *impact* of Social Security *taxation* on your future. This can be done only if we can look at the 'big-picture,' meaning where you are now and precisely where you will be with predictable, countable assets. I'm not saying you won't pick the right horse in the Kentucky Derby, but in my office we deal only in current facts.

Also, people planning to take early Social Security retirement benefits should be most interested in the effect on benefits if they plan to "work in retirement" as they receive those early benefits. Your benefit may be penalized (reduced) depending on how much you make during your early-benefit period . . . one more reason to look at early SSA benefits with both eyes wide open!

You would no longer be subject to benefit reductions once you reach your designated Full Retirement Age. You would be able to earn as much as possible without having to worry about penalties against your benefits.

(For more information, go to http//assets.arp.org/rgcenter/econ/boomers_envition_1.pdf)

If Social Security "Cost of Working in Retirement" penalties sound incidental, know that for every $3 you earn when taking benefits *less than a year* before you reach your FRA, the Social Security Administration will deduct $1 from your benefit for every $3 earned above your earnings limit! If you file early and take benefits *one year or more* before your Full Retirement Age, the Social Security Administration deducts $1 of every $2 you make over $15,480.

Either way, when filing early, not only do you stand to lose more than 50% of your total benefits for life, your early-retirement benefits stand to be cut in half, as well (this applies to every dollar earned over $15,480, at this writing). So . . . what's the point of filing early? You would lose too much money, in my opinion, when all you have to do is wait a handful of years to file at the right time. THIS is where it makes a lot of sense to have other instruments in place, instruments that will fill your EARLY-retirement income gap.

Call it "Now Versus Later" income. Call it whatever you like. I hope I've made my point about taking early benefits. I also hope that you can now see the incredible advantage of waiting until age 70 to receive extended benefits. For many people, this will be the very cornerstone of their retirement future. This is where you maximize your retirement income for life and this is how to increase your survivor benefits. If you are still healthy and capable of working, why not plan on increasing your Social Security benefits in order to create a bigger, more sustainable income for the rest of your days?

If you fail to delay, the "Now Versus Later" equation still stands: You still need income. Now you will need even more income from some other source!

Consider the Source . . .

People needing early benefits may come to me for other reasons: They may be in poor health, they may have a drastically reduced life expectancy, they also might be living in fear of day-to-day living expenses . . . OR, they have been given *the wrong information.*

Either way, if anyone tries to talk you - or anyone you know - into taking early Social Security benefits, have them talk to me, first! For most people, I have alternatives that can replace early benefits and save them hundreds of thousands of dollars in income over a lifetime. You absolutely MUST take a good, hard look at the LONG-TERM when it comes to "Now Versus Later" income.

As you consider the long-term potential of your retirement years, everyone reading this book should be asking one important question: "Exactly how long WILL I LIVE in retirement?" This is an issue many people would rather avoid. Some people hope to go out in a blaze of glory like Thelma and Louise. But let's get real. A reasonably healthy, 65-year-old man is now expected to live until age 92 . . . that's 27 more years! His wife will live until 94, statistically speaking, or 29 more years, this according to figures from 2012 report by the Society of Actuaries.

To put a face on it, think of a couple named "Rob" and "Laura" who lived and thrived in their 20s - back in the early 60s – and people just like this are still with us today, in 2015! YES, life is long and getting longer. Don't just plan *on* it, plan *for* it.

It is up to you to decide *when* to file and *how* to file. I can help you make that vitally important decision. After all, this is one of the most important parts of the "big picture." While publications like *Smart Money* and *Money Magazine* go into various ways to score on Wall Street or how to increase the value of their homes for down-sizing – none of which is bad advice - the importance and the mechanisms of Social Security are rarely emphasized. Now that you've had a look at some of the little-known facts, let me help you go after the benefits you deserve.

CHAPTER NINE

Power-Up Your Bottom Line

W E'VE TALKED ABOUT inside-tips for negotiating the Social Security maze. You have seen why it makes good financial sense for anyone to wait for benefits until your FRA – which is currently age 66 for people born between 1943 and 1954 – and that's great. And I have yet another little secret to pass on, which can add to your SSA benefits:

By now, I'll bet *you think* you know what I'm about to say: that by delaying benefits until age 70, if both spouses delay until age 70, that you would have done everything possible to maximize your Social Security. Good. But, you would be wrong. Here's something people don't know: If *both* spouses delay benefits until 70, they could be *losing more than $135,000*! Surprise again.

I'll spare you the details on this one for the moment. I could probably dedicate another book to the topic of Social Security benefits, alone. For now, just know that among dozens of possible *benefit-age-election* combinations, one will be the best for you. I'm sure of it. I'm also quite certain that I can help you properly analyze every option appropriate for your situation. With very few exceptions, I have been able to make a real difference in the retirement lives of hundreds of people -to the tune of not just thousands but *hundreds of thousands* of dollars.

It should be clear by now that the decisions you make pertaining to how you "elect" to take your Social Security will be some of the MOST IMPORTANT decisions you ever make. Considering what I have seen, I'd say that the difference between the best Social Security-election decisions often amount to $100,000, $200,000 . . . even up to $300,000, or more, in benefits you would receive for *the rest of your life!*

Paying Forward, Giving Back

How do I benefit directly from helping you maximize your Social Security benefits? I don't. But I still consider it one of the most important things I do. When appropriate, I help people with additional opportunities in the form of Fixed Index Annuities and other innovative and traditional products from the insurance industry, and I do make commissions, so that's the monetary payoff for me – but only if it would be a significant payoff for *you*.

If you have read anything about me, if you have listened to any of my radio shows, if you have read any of my other books in addition to this one, then *you know* what I am all about: In my first book, titled *Don't Die Broke* (Agate Publishers, 2009), I said it's "not always about the money." This is true in business and it is true in life. If I hadn't adopted this philosophy early on in my career, I am convinced that my business would be nowhere near as successful as it is today.

Success in life is all about 'paying forward' and 'giving back,' in my opinion. I began in the insurance industry at a time when salespeople were pressured into pushing just one kind of product – a product that provided fairly minimal benefits for customers while creating big profits for the insurance company. I quickly removed myself from that kind of business culture, entirely, because I knew that such an approach would lead to either change or failure. It always does.

I went on alone with the idea that I would build my business on trust, putting the customer's well-being at the top of my list of priorities. This is why the book you have in your hands right now is full of so many valuable, little-known secrets, things you can put to use with me or without me to maximize your Social Security income. In other words, I wanted this book to be for *you*, about *you*, and not about me. I did this because I know you've probably read other books about retirement planning. I know that most, if not all, of those books push some sort of product at the consumer, while few to none offer anything beyond a self-serving agenda.

I hope you'll remember that when you pass this book along to your friends and loved ones. Yes, I am in business to make money. No, I do not do business at the expense of people I plan to call friends for years to come. It truly is "All About *You*" in my office, which is why I'm still here and thriving after so many years - while other planners have, frankly, gone down the tubes.

When it comes to planning the best possible outcome for your retirement, please give me a chance to prove the value of my strategies. My name is David Reindel and you know where to find me: **My phone number is 888-639-5113 or (direct) 860-245-0633**. I chose my office location deliberately, wanting it to be a pleasant place to visit and an inspirational setting for people in or nearing retirement. I'm in an intimate and picturesque part of beautiful Mystic, Connecticut, which, in itself, is worth a visit.

We all look forward to seeing you walk through the door. For many, that moment is the first step into a world of retirement bliss. I want this experience to be the same for you. Until then . . .

CHAPTER TEN

Tracking the Missing Link

NOW THAT WE'VE established all sorts of ways to maximize your Social Security income, let's look at other things that will 'ensure' more income. I have the answer in the form of what I call "The Missing Link." And from here it's not about "ensuring" more income. It's about "INsuring" more income.

This is important. This is "huge," as they say. For anyone with the ability to take the next step, please pay careful attention to this chapter because the solutions you are about to see are some of the best, in my opinion.

Since the crash, the 'great recession' and now the near-runaway market recovery period, all kinds of new versions of traditional solutions have popped up. Some claim to be "insurance hybrids" offering unlimited upside market potential with none of the down, and so forth. But know this: My industry has exploded since the market was exposed for what it really is. We now know that a risk environment is a world without remorse for retiree losses.

As a direct response to widespread alarm among retirees, the insurance industry has responded, in kind, with hundreds of variations of what essentially amounts to "retirement insurance." Each of the hundreds of variations may come with dozens of features, like proverbial "variations on a theme." But not all may be right for you and your retirement time line.

I have used my decades of professional experience to narrow the playing field to a select and strategic pick of the best in the orchard. These are insurance products, to be sure, with options and features that really work, and work well for my clients. You can meet with any number of other advisors and let them run you through the gauntlet of products out there. In fact, I always suggest that people get a second opinion. If you have any concerns, and simply want to test the waters, go ahead and shop around.

Then come back to me for another look because I've run every product through my own formula of mathematical calculations. I have seen the results of certain options offered by others in the insurance business. I can pass along one fairly obvious conclusion right now: some options and features work better than others. But all of them must pass the "personality test," meaning, do they personally fit *you* and who *you* are . . . and where *you* need to be in the next 5, 10, 20 or 30 years down the road?

Rebuilding Bygone Pensions: The Missing Link "Foundation"

Now it's time to take things a step beyond Social Security, the cornerstone for your own self-designed pension plan. If Social Security is a cornerstone, I am now going to provide the "missing link" to the virtual *foundation* for your retirement income.

Most retirees were forced long ago to trade pension plans for Qualified Contribution plans – meaning 401Ks and the rest. Adding Social Security to the "missing link" can create a very viable alternative, of course, and if you have a traditional pension that's great. I wish you the best. My alternative 'pension-like' set of formulas can give you a powerful additive to fuel your existing pension plan.

The New 'Self-Pension' Plan

A majority of retirees probably don't, or won't, have company pensions. As you may know, traditional pension models have been challenged by increasing longevity among their pensioners. But that's not the only challenge. I refer to a 2011 report from a community newspaper in my area, *The Fairfield Citizen*, of Fairfield, Connecticut, which announced that required **employee contributions** to the local police and fire pension plan would have to **triple** over a five-year period running through 2016 – in order to help keep this traditional pension model afloat.

This is a symptom of problems with traditional pensions today.

The problem in Fairfield had to do with the rate of inflation versus returns on town earnings from its investments. Something like that. But reading between the lines, "inflation" – which hasn't really kicked in just yet – is a stepson of longevity and retirees are living longer, so pension structures must change accordingly. Either way - and for whatever reason at the bottom line of the ledger – Fairfield PD and Fire employees were asked to dig deeper into their own pockets.

This is nothing new. I suspect inflation and longevity projections are working against traditional pension designs nationwide. Most were replaced long ago with matching-contribution plans in 401Ks and the like, but how much can you *afford* to contribute when other alternatives make more sense, mathematically speaking? My 'self-pension' solutions offer excellent alternatives to troubled and vanishing pension plans, and uncertain market investment packages.

Let's look at how we analyze the latter in the New Millennium of Retirement Planning:

Beware of the Antiquated 4% Rule

If you want to find out whether or not someone has been watching for danger signs in their retirement plan, just ask them how it works. If they mutter something about the "4% Rule," you're talking to someone behind the curve.

For years – some of which saw little change in market returns – the shopworn axiom called for retirees to live on a 4% annual withdrawal from their investment portfolios. Such portfolios were in the market, of course, and that's the way many retirees lived until half their portfolios died . . . those portfolios were virtually wiped out during the "lost decade."

Believe it or not, many advisors still try to cling to the old 4% Rule. Their clients accordingly stand to suffer a failure rate of more than 50% . . . yes, even in this booming market recovery, according to a well-respected study by Michael Finke, who heads the Personal Finance Program at Texas Tech University. Finke and colleagues Wade Pfau and David Blanchett released their 2013 findings citing the hazards of relying on 4% withdrawals from market accounts in a "Low-Yield world."

Four-Percenters Make a 'Grave Mistake'

They go on to say that advisors make a "grave mistake" when trying to gauge the future success of client portfolios on the past history of market performance. For years, advisors considered the history of market performance a virtual guarantee that results would remain the same in the future. This, supported by a Wharton School of Business study and longer-term snapshots per the CAPE Shiller-Barclay index, show that expectations of 'more of the same' signal potential doom for the 4% Rule . . . and for those investors, those who stick to it.

Nowadays more than a few investors realize that 20th Century market results hardly predict what will happen on Wall Street in the 21st Century. Why would they? It also stands to reason that if someone continues to rely on the old 4% Rule of withdrawal - from a retirement portfolio 100% marinated in market investments – they will very likely *run out of money* in a retirement spanning 30 years. In other words, old models supported with bygone historical data of another era won't hold up. They have no real correlation to the dynamic outlined earlier in this book. They have nothing to do with factors facing retirees today, especially those nearing or new to retirement.

Economists specifically warn that heavy market losses in an early-retirement investment portfolio have a particularly significant impact on potential failure in later years. Our hapless 4-percenter might argue that, "I'm mostly in bonds." Yes, but the old withdrawal-rule is based on antiquated 8.6% average market returns. Unfortunately for old models, the market returned an average of just above 5% during the "lost decade." The 4% Rule also still relies on an antiquated 2.6% average return, Fiske noted in 2013, while bond yields came up 4% short of the mark in that year.

Sure, you might argue that things have improved at this writing, but that isn't quite the point. As you have already learned from earlier Sequence of Returns-Risk models, the downward pull on a market portfolio occurs due to lost bits, and bites, over different periods of time, followed by recovery periods, followed by more bites out of your bottom line. If calibrated over a five-year period through January 2013, the bond failure rate leapt to a disturbing 57%. . . . So much for relying on bond-layered strategies.

If you think you can afford to weather a 4% portfolio withdrawal plan through low-interest periods, and come out ahead, stay in. But you should know that New Millennium analysts warn that the old 4% model can no longer be trusted as being a safe-haven for your money. Using updated equations, the most important finding by Fiske and colleagues is that the 4% Rule led to an actual loss/failure rate of more than 50% in *bond* portfolios.

Risk is RISK

Throughout the pages of all of my other books, I have always said that *risk is risk*. Bonds are in the market. Bonds are at risk. Municipalities defaulted on bonds during the recession. Nothing is sacred in this coliseum. Yet, people still say, "We'll I'm in *bonds*" – as if to indicate that no greater safety can be had for one's retirement savings. Hah! Next, this individual will assure you that his "bonds will go up again . . . always do." Who could argue with that? Of course they will . . . until they stop and go down. But how long can *you* wait for recovery in retirement? That's the point!

The riveting factor in the Fiske study is that even if bonds recover over a five-year period, they still lose 18%, which is still considered more than three-times what the old 4% models considered acceptable. If the recovery of your bond portfolio needs a 10-year recovery period, your rate of "failure" would be upwards of 32%! Thus, a low-yield market can be a "retirement income game changer," Fiske concludes, noting that those who rely on "20th century market returns . . . we may never see again" are living with a "false sense of security."

(Sources include: Fink, Pfau, Blanchett study, Texas Tech; ThinkAdvisor.com 1/17/13)

Annuities Deserve "Another Look"

For those who doubt the staying power and dependability of annuities, our Texas Tech analysts suggest that you look again. They say advisors, and their investors who remain "stuck in the past," may not want to give up *potential* yields of which they've become accustomed. Are they kidding themselves? What about the historic losses investors have already endured?

The new smart-money is based on the understanding that you can overestimate risk-based returns, and that retirees can annuitize instruments that offer guaranteed returns in down markets of all kinds. Analysts and economists now know the truth: Pre-retirees - and retirees in particular - must minimize risk. They must adopt a more conservative route to income-planning in retirement. This means something more than taking a "magic pill" in the form of tacking on more market risk. If you do, *do not* blame the market if you stay in too long to recover your losses for a safe retirement.

Let's Get Real

The market "is what it *is*." I've said it before. Market-play is for younger investors. You are making a mistake, right now, if you are beyond 55 and your money has too much market exposure. Let's get real: You want safeguards against disastrous losses. You need the kind of "longevity" protection I've been talking about in this book. You also need to plan for liquidity for emergencies. Although the newer annuities offer more liquidity, we'll look at your situation to determine how much *you* actually need. In some cases, a rider can provide additional liquidity. To offset the risk of catastrophic illness, long-term care insurance also might be useful – if you are of a certain age and can qualify.

Many a boomer today sees retirement as more of a nightmare than a dream. But it's time to turn that outlook around. Start by making a real study of your household expenses. Know exactly where your money goes every month, each week if necessary. How much goes down the drain with non-essential expenses like premier movie channels and extra smart phones? Have you tried to plan for taxation of your retirement income?

If you're in the "boomer zone" age-wise, like I am, please know that 40 percent of people in retirement today have *under*-estimated the length of time they will spend on this earth, this according to a study by the accounting firm Ernst & Young. From 2000 to 2013 the market came up near-empty handed in terms of gains, winding up close to where it began. Still, market investors unfortunately had to foot the bill for those pricey investment fees, which, for some investors, ran as high as 3% a year – leading investors into negative territory . . . meaning they *lost* money through the "lost decade" at a time when they absolutely should have been steadily increasing their savings. Tragic. Truly, truly tragic.

Vanquish the Lies: Annuity Facts vs Fiction

So much for the past. Looking forward, let's face facts: ***Annuities are more consumer-friendly than ever! Annuities are more widely popular than ever before!*** I want you to toss aside all those propaganda-driven misconceptions (often outright lies) spread with such ruthless abandon before the crash:

- **Forget about lies insisting that all annuities are "bad."** Varieties of annuities number in the hundreds with countless features and more flexibility than ever before!

- **Annuities are not the perfect solution for all people**.

- **The best annuity candidates are people in or near retirement** with a low risk tolerance!

- **Forget about annuities being limited to things like SPIAs.** The Single Premium Immediate Annuity has been around a long time. People assume when they envision "annuities" that you get an income stream for a certain time period, as a trade-off for a lump sum of cash. Insurance carriers have no idea how much this instrument could earn over a certain time period. You cannot put a price on this instrument in terms of maximum earnings. And if you try to make lots of money with a SPIA, forget it – that's not how it works.

- **The best way to build interest-earnings is through a broad range of "deferred annuities,"** meaning that your earnings grow and compound without risk of being lost when markets drop.

- **Fixed annuities are not "investments,"** they are insurance products. So, don't try to compare them to market "investments," which can give you an overnight-killing, sure, but they can also kill your savings *overnight*.

- **Annuities protect principal and grow steadily,** a strategy that has been shown to equal or exceed long-term investments left to market risk.

- **Do not expect to get rich with annuities.** They come with guarantees. They mirror life insurance in that they insure against "longevity risk" and premature death.

- **Annuities are not expensive** in their fundamentally "fixed" form. A basic fixed annuity lacking features like an income rider might come entirely without fees. Add death benefits and other features and they may add an annual fee, but often less than 1%.

Your Financial Keystone: The Fixed Indexed Annuity

When people mistakenly talk about so-called "hybrid" annuities, it's a misnomer. The term "hybrid" applies to a separate investment class altogether.

But none of those come close to the Fixed Indexed Annuity: This is a very specifically designed class of "annuity" and it comes with particularly powerful features. It IS related to the market, in that it can be attached to investment earnings made by the insurance company. Yet, the Fixed Indexed Annuity is essentially "insured" against loss.

Unlike a "variable" annuity product, assets in a Fixed Indexed Annuity *cannot be lost* when the market takes a nose-dive into the deep end of a bad economy. Having the best aspects of a variable product, the Fixed Indexed Annuity shares in market gains made through insurance carrier investments . . . in the market. The insurance company eats the risk. You take your winnings safely home . . . for life.

Index activity in a given year does affect earnings of a Fixed Indexed Annuity. Index gains determine how much you get. But at no time during the year would the money in your FIA account actually be placed in the market as an investment. Your money would *never* be at risk on Wall Street.

With a **Fixed Indexed Annuity** you can sit back, relax and know that *you can make money without losing money*!

This is going to be YOUR MONEY . . . for the rest of your life . . . MAKE IT, DON'T RISK IT!

You will do much better than people in simple fixed annuities earning 1% to 3%. That's another rampant misnomer propagated by risk advocates: *Fixed Indexed Annuities are related to, but very different than, fixed annuities.* You can see *very nice, respectable earnings with Fixed Indexed Annuities.*

Insure Those Treacherous Early Years in Retirement

Let's look at a quick check-list of where we've been so far:

- *You're considering a new approach to Social Security (or already taking benefits).*

- *You have other investments to beef up your monthly income, but they are still at risk.*

- *You like the idea of increasing principal through FIA earnings, but we haven't met.*

- *You haven't made the decision to move forward on any of the above.*

If this is you, and if you are anywhere between age 55 and 65, you are in the Retiree Danger Zone. I'm talking about the period of time leading up to your retirement, also the often financially-fatal moment *soon after* people retire. This is the time when your retirement investments absolutely must be protected while being allowed to bring in as much as possible . . . mess this up and you may be forced to survive on Social Security alone!

Imagine the poor guy who had just taken the gold watch in August, 2008. He retired with assets in some IRA or 401(k) plan, only to see half of his portfolio go up in smoke with the autumn leaves of October '08. The real problem was the loss of his long-term ability to earn steady, reliable returns on his principal . . . for the rest of his life. His earnings ability was cut in half!

As you move through retirement in something like a Fixed Indexed Annuity . . .

- ***Your money keeps on growing.***

- ***You build up a war chest as you age.***

- *You actually MAKE MONEY, growing your principal*

- *You will be comfortable financially for the rest of your days.*

Otherwise, your early retirement nest-egg faces serious corrosion from Sequence of Returns Risk. This is what happened to boomers during the 'lost decade.' This is what happened to most retirees. You DO NOT want to be exposed to SOR because the facts are in: The best thing that can happen to a market investor is NOTHING. Market investors hope nothing unruly happens in the market for a period of 10 to 15 years, giving his market investments time to grow, thus allowing his principal to strengthen into a real retirement war chest.

Unfortunately this rarely happens, if ever.

Things DO happen in the market, bad things, and when they do, studies by some of the most astute experts in the world clearly show that *investors in retirement with money in the market* may very well *run OUT of money* before they die.

A Suit of Armor for Your Money

Think of a Fixed Index Annuity as way to put an *insurance suit of armor* around your money in a market-*related* instrument. You will be protected against Sequence of Returns Risk because the insurance company assumes that risk. Now, why would they be willing to stick their necks out, allowing you to make money while they assume all the risk? Good question . . . I'll explain shortly.

For now, know that you can create an income stream with your Fixed Indexed Annuity. You will protect your principal investment, no matter what happens. You will be able to move forward into retirement with earnings, not loss. It's like having a team of advisors manage your risk in diversified investments on *your* behalf, without putting *your* money at risk!

An Old 'Risk-Alternative'

It's up to you. Most market advisors have learned to do what popular personal-finance magazines wrote about for decades: They would take your money and put it into 'diversified' forms of risk, do their best to manage the risk on your behalf, and hope for the best . . . but it's still your money, all of it . . . not a single cent comes out of the advisor's bank account.

When market waters became choppy and dangerously volatile in the past, a market advisor could hardly provide income guarantees. All he could do was try to pull your money out in time, to leave enough intact in order to rebuild your financial future. They couldn't guarantee income in your retirement. They still can't. YOU CAN.

- **What you cannot afford - at any point in your retirement - to allow your money to lose 20% to 30% in value, or more!**

- **You must lock-in principal.**

- **Locked-in, earned interest must be added to your compounding pool of retirement income.**

- **You must have an instrument in place that protects the latest "high-water mark" of your earnings from loss.**

- **You must continue to generate earnings in this manner throughout the remaining years of your retirement.**

You can do this with a Fixed Indexed Annuity!

We now have yet another version of the FIA called the "contingent deferred annuity," which allows you to remove the insurance wrapper after a number of years in the "Retiree Safe Zone," after the tumultuous market gales are behind you. But that's one of many topics left for meetings in my office.

For the abbreviated purposes of this book, let's move on . . .

CHAPTER ELEVEN

FIA Power:
. . . Pure and Simple

LET'S TALK ABOUT Fixed Indexed Annuities (FIAs) from the inside-out, casting a spotlight on the internal workings of this highly versatile tool. Introducing the FIA and how it works . . .

The Power of Guaranteed Indexing

At its most fundamental heart, the Fixed Indexed Annuity is a contract between you and an insurance company. Yet, unlike more traditional annuities, the FIA is connected to a market index. These indexes, otherwise known as "indices," include the DOW, the S&P 500 and others, and this is where securities are bought and sold.

Before the Fixed Indexed Annuity came along, traditional fixed annuities required a lump sum investment. The insurance company set a rate of interest which was "fixed" like a bank savings account, although without the shifting interest rates. These annuities are around today and still give the contract owner earned interest for a time, at a fixed rate. The accumulated value of the account inside a fixed annuity must eventually be distributed. Yet, simple 'fixed annuities' have been criticized for giving annuity owners low earnings accumulated through low interest rates.

More and more investors began to demand something more. People wanted the dependability of a fixed annuity, including the same guaranteed principal AND with market participation. They wanted to earn more money without having to risk the loss of previous gains. In other words, they wanted their increased earnings "locked in."

Insurance companies heard the call and worked hard to come up with something besides the sometimes notorious "variable" annuity – think of a mutual fund packaged with certain features of an annuity.

The world was ready for something new, a new product with a previously unthinkable combination of win-win features for the consumer. The Fixed Indexed Annuity was born. The elementals of the FIA work like this: If a market index linked to an indexed annuity goes up, the annuity holder enjoys a piece of the earnings made by the insurance company. If the market takes another dive, the annuity contract holder loses nothing because the insurance carrier has assumed all the risk!

Reliable, Dependable Fixed Indexed Annuities!

Those insurance companies able to offer Fixed Indexed Annuities tend to be some of the world's strongest companies. The companies I work with have been in business for more than a century in some cases. They have an accordingly enormous powerhouse of financial resources. In other words they WILL recover from market drops. They will be there for you because they have – and they have always had - both the time and money to withstand markets. YOU don't. YOU can, however, become part of this awesome investment powerhouse and share a portion of their gain, say, 6% to 8% or more, in an up-market environment. When the S&P plummets – and it will – you and your Fixed Indexed Annuity will be able to sit it out until the index recovers and begins to rise all over again – and it will!

Some people think I'm a pessimist when it comes to markets and investing, but I'm not. Not at all. I'm just a mathematical realist. This is precisely why I advocate Fixed Indexed Annuities for retirees.

You've seen the historic numbers in this book. What goes up must come down . . . and what went down *will* go up again. The stock market is no different. I simply protect my clients against a time in life when they've run out of time for the downs. This is the time when they need only ups – to stay firmly on the upside, to keep moving forward, not backward – no matter what happens elsewhere in the world.

- **Fixed Indexed Annuities create additional earning potential when times are good**

- **Fixed Indexed Annuities guarantee the safety of your principal**

- **Fixed Indexed Annuities protect the money you make**

- **Fixed Indexed Annuities ensure that you cannot lose what you've already made**

- **Fixed Indexed Annuities create greater earnings than standard fixed annuities**

FIXED INDEXED ANNUITIES ARE THE VERY BEST, SAFE-MONEY ALTERNATIVE!

This is my opinion, obviously, but I've been in this industry longer than almost anyone you can name. I'm licensed to offer securities, as well. I could offer you stocks and bonds and make commissions for myself, but I can't do that unless I first urge you to look at Fixed Indexed Annuities. I feel this way because I am convinced that Fixed Indexed Annuities are absolutely among the finest class of investment products available in the world today.

Rumors Denied:
Few to No "Fees and Charges" with FIAs

Let's take a quick run-down of how the FIA functions versus other annuities: Again, indexed annuities run much like other annuities, yet instead of growing your money at a fixed interest rate – often set from the beginning by the insurance company and set for the life of the contract – the growth of a Fixed Indexed Annuity is linked to a designated market index. You have enormous additional upside potential, without risk of losing your gains or principal.

Now, about those much rumored and misunderstood so-called "fees and charges" associated with annuities in general: You cannot generalize when looking at annuities. While we've touched on fees associated with some annuities, I need to stress that Fixed Indexed Annuities are rarely plagued by the fees associated with other instruments. In fact, **with most Fixed Indexed Annuity products, it would be rare to see any fees** deducted from your account.

When people hear about "annuity fees," such fees are often associated with "variable annuities." Variable annuities tend to come with a variety of charges and fees, and they tend to increase when you add features including optional riders. If the variable annuity has underlying "sub-accounts," these may carry their own array of charges, as well, adding up to around 1% annually. If you then want to add a death-benefit rider or income rider, fees for such options may be up to 4% per year with a variable annuity. Even basic fees associated with variables can add up quickly and include items like Mortality and Expense Risk Charges, along with various administrative fees, which can cost around 1.4% a year.

Again, Fixed Indexed Annuities rarely come with fees attached.

Financial instruments play different roles in the lives of retirees. Life insurance is essentially meant to provide a lump-sum payout to beneficiaries upon the death of the policy holder. Health insurance is there to help with medical bills. Savings accounts hold emergency cash, while checking accounts are used to handle periodic and monthly bills.

Annuities and Lifetime Income

Income annuities create income. The primary design of an income annuity provides for either immediate income or income received at some future point in time. It's really that simple. You can put a lump sum into an 'income' annuity and expect to receive *ongoing income*.

If you wouldn't need that income immediately, the "roll-up" function takes effect, meaning that your annuity can grow at a certain rate, for a certain number of years, or until you start taking income out of the annuity. An annuity with a roll-up feature can grow the value of your lifetime income by a set amount, which can be comforting in retirement because . . . these products are designed to generate income for more than just a few years – *they can create a guaranteed stream of income for a lifetime.* Now, add in the indexing power of an FIA.

Life-long Income and FIAs

The "lifetime income" capability of a Fixed Indexed 'Income' Annuity makes this type of product one of the most popular among retirees today. We have covered income riders, the value of having a fixed rate of compounding interest, and the power of indexing ensured to protect your money. Now, add the income feature and you can see why I get excited about this solution for so many of my clients. It is simply hard to beat in today's uncertain world of risk versus reward.

FIA Returns . . . *'Forever'*

While Fixed Indexed Annuities will give you a portion of market gains made by the insurance company, such gains may vary. While you cannot lose what you make, the gains are based on the Wall Street roller coaster. UNLIKE variable annuities, you cannot lose money in a declining market with a Fixed Indexed Annuity. UNLIKE variable annuities, laddered bonds, asset-allocated-diversified stock packages and layered mutual fund strategies . . . with Fixed Indexed Annuities, your earnings continue and *never consume your principal.*

I have seen people lose lots of money after their advisors put them into variable annuities, stocks, bonds and mutual funds. Variable Annuities, like other risk instruments, may offer higher returns in upside markets, but they are no different than stocks and mutual funds in terms of risk – they are all exposed to risk.

Never once have I had one of my clients lose money in a Fixed Indexed Annuity. My clients MAKE money. They don't RISK money.

They love the life-long REWARD of being financially safe while living carefree, independent retirement lifestyles with Fixed Indexed Annuities.

An Up-and-Down Waltz with Risk

Let's take a quick look at a couple of $250,000 investments pumped into the market in the Year 2000. Follow the 13-year cycle of these investments through 2013 and watch what happens: During the first year, the S&P declined by 10.14%, leaving our 'risk' account with $224,650 – after the very first year out of the gate. And the trend continued with another $13.04% drop on the S&P in 2001, followed by yet another drop – more like a mini-crash – when the S&P took a $23.37% nosedive. After only three years in the market, our $250,000 market investment was down to $149,701. Then came the upward climb, as usual, adding back $26.38% the following year, followed by 8.99% in the next, then and 3% in 2005, followed by 13.62% in 2006 and 3.53% in 2007. The account was finally back up to . . . can you guess? It was back up to "zero"! It was back to 'basis,' with a value of $249,832, after all those supposed "recovery" years.

We all know what happened next – the Crash of '08 – and this particular account was back down to $153,672, almost overnight, practically speaking. When the subsequent recovery era finally took off, this account saw a 23.44% increase in 2009 and the trend almost continued with a 12.78% rise in 2010, only to flat-line at less than a 1% gain in 2011 (actually plus-0.02%), regaining traction again in 2012 and 2013, with 13.41% and 29.60% increases respectively for those years.

The market account value in the end, after all those crazy years, wound up at only $315,069.

Do those reeling numbers make your head spin? They have that effect on mine and that's why I've presented them here! If you were in the market through that tumultuous era, trying to keep track of the ups and downs of this particular market account, you would have had a lot of sleepless nights. That's the net-effect of risk.

The Short, Sweet Story of FA Compounding

In comparison, here's the long-and-short story of a simple 'Fixed' Annuity account, which covers the same market over the same time period: It was set to grow and compound at 3% per year through the entire period. In the end, it had a value of *$378,147.* End of story. This simple, fixed annuity overtook, overpowered, and basically overwhelmed the market account above and all its promises of untold wealth. Sitting calmly on the sidelines and accumulating compounded interest, it beat the market account by *$63,078.*

I can put the net-effect on a chart. Let's call it "What Happens When You are Not Prepared." The chart would simply show that a 40.1% drop between 2000 and 2002 would require a 67.0% recovery . . . *to break even.* The 38.5% dive in account value in 2008 would demand a 62.7% total rebound . . . *just to break even.*

This is a hypothetical illustration but the numbers and their effects on the potential value on a market account are quite real. Ignore the mathematical laws of The Rule of 100, and cumulative market risk will catch up with you.

That said, if you have an IRA or some other Qualified Plan, how much of your money is vulnerable to market risk in that plan? Risk can ruin your plans in retirement! The Rule of 100 dictates that a 65-year-old should have *no more than* 35% of her savings "at risk" in the market. When I mean "risk," I'm talking about stocks, bonds, REITs (Real Estate Investment Trusts), oil and gas investments, index mutual funds, and anything else based on stock market investments.

When I mean "safety," I'm talking about checking and savings accounts, fixed annuities, money markets, CDs, treasuries and . . . Fixed Indexed Annuities. Taking any other course through the rest of your retirement years could mean risking your retirement nest egg. As for your Qualified Contribution accounts, I can show you how to get maximum performance out of those IRA and 401k monies. Regardless where your money may be at any given time, if you are anywhere near or in "The Retirement Zone" you need to pick up the phone and give me a call. You wouldn't be the last one in the world to wait too long and lose an important opportunity to maximize a lifetime source of steady income.

With Fixed Indexed Annuities You Enjoy . . .

- *Gain without loss*
- *No Loss in a market crash . . . you go into idle-mode (as variables and stocks keep losing!)*
- *A Certain Level of Interest grows in the Fixed Indexed Annuity, even in idle-mode*

Fixed Indexed Annuities have excellent potential for strong earnings in market upcycles, some returning up to 15 percent or more in recent years. Here's how it works: Should the Dow return 20% in a strong year, meaning that the insurance company earns 20 percent on its investments, in this example you would get 15 percent. *No, you don't get it all*, but what a miniscule price to pay for watching your insurance carrier take all the risk – especially if the DOW plummets 25% the following year, annihilating all of last year's gains as it keeps on going DOWN, devouring yet another 5% below the lost 20% . . . which would have taken a 5% bite out of your bottom-line principal - had you been in variables, stocks, bonds, mutual funds.

I posed the question earlier as to why the insurance company allows you to increase principal with your having to share the risk. As you can see in the scenario above, the insurance company gets to keep 5% of the 20% you would have made in the market, had your money been wholly exposed to risk. The insurance company keeps 5% of the 20% gain on the DOW. You get 15%. But you do not lose 25% the following year. As I said: a small price to pay. This is why the insurance company allows you to earn while it eats your risk!

And all the while, even after losing heavily in down-markets, *risk accounts still have to shell out fees and administrative costs*. Yet, risk advocates dare call FIAs "expensive." Who are they kidding?

CHAPTER TWELVE

Grow Your $$ with Survival Tools

D URING THE DOWNTURN illustrated in the last chapter, your Fixed Indexed Annuity would protect your contracted percentage of gain from the prior year, the good year when the market was up 20% and you earned 15%. As the market collapsed 25% the following year, you would just sit tight, with all of the money you made to that point safely tucked away with your uninterrupted, guaranteed income stream if you have an upcoming feature called an "Income Rider."

A History of Peace of Mind

In this book, I've already presented actual year-by-year, historic data from the Wall Street roller coaster. After riding through hell-and-high water in an era when Wall Street investors made roughly *the same amount of gain* as those holding Fixed Indexed Annuity contracts, remember the Peace of Mind Factor.

People with Fixed Income Annuities made it through without lost sleep and Wall Street brain damage. And here's something else to think about when it comes to the Peace of Mind Factor: No two historic periods are exactly alike, as economists in the last chapter so astutely point out. What if Wall Street gains will be less overall in the future than they were in the "lost decade"? Can you afford to wait and find out? If you are 55 or older you cannot.

Consider Facts, not "Forecasts"

Classic, standard fixed annuities were popular among pensioners living in *ancient Rome*. Traditional fixed annuities ensured steady retirement income through the centuries for pensioners in the *British Empire*. Those were archaic annuities. Now consider the earning power and flexibility of modern fixed annuities, which still guarantee principal, even offering a minimum guarantee of interest. Standard fixed annuities might offer somewhat higher levels of "fixed" interest, because they get no part of carrier earnings when the S&P soars.

Now look at the best of all worlds: Fixed Indexed Annuities. FIAs offer the baseline guarantees of some standard fixed annuities – while STILL offering an impressive share of gain on a given index. What more could anyone want as we face the impact of uncertain economies worldwide?

The 'Non-Liquidity' Myth

The oft-debated issue of "liquidity" comes up when talking about annuities, but know that if carriers-across-the-board once charged annuity contract holders heavy penalties for early withdrawal . . . things . . . HAVE . . . changed!

These days, most annuities offer liberal thresholds of annual withdrawals of 10% of account value per year, or more, no questions asked. Some allow more. In fact, carriers are offering increasingly consumer-friendly withdrawal penalties – some are even offering *penalty-free* withdrawals along with other liquidity options.

A Cautionary Note:

One note of caution: It is of the utmost importance to have a truly experienced annuity expert on your side. Before you make any decision related to these potentially complex instruments, know the professional background of the advisor sitting across the desk. Work with an *inexperienced* advisor and you will face either a mind-boggling array of variation – which he doesn't seem to fully grasp – OR, you will see a single, my-way-or-the-highway product dropped in front of you. I know.

I've seen the long faces of people who have come to me for help AFTER making serious mistakes. They didn't know to come to me, first, but you do. You now know I was there when things like Fixed Indexed Annuities were introduced. I've been there through the changes. I can talk about a wide array of products and features from experience and sheer memory . . . when other planners fumble through pages of carrier guidebooks, hunting for answers to your questions.

When delving into this powerful, yet misunderstood corner of the investment universe, you need an annuity expert like me, not a neophyte in the annuity world. Many such advisors have appeared out of the woodwork – ever since Fixed Indexed Annuities became all-the-rage among smart-money investors at the dawn of the Great Recession. You'll know you're dealing with a "neophyte" when the advisor is forced to excuse himself in order to dive into a carrier manual, one too many times.

Lifetime Income: the Modern Miracle

By now, you know the crucial importance of having a lifetime-income guarantee. This type of guarantee has become one of the most popular of all annuity features since the recession. Of course! Having a lifetime income from an annuity can protect you from being a front-door greeter at a big-box retail store . . . *in your 80s.*

Not all annuities have lifetime income options and you will find a lot of variation with income riders. For example, you get income for a period of time with some. Your annuity can also provide an income stream for a loved one after you die. If you need to fill the Income Gap before Social Security benefits begin, income riders can do just that. Income Riders can be invaluable when planning Spousal Benefit strategies and certain tax advantages are available as well.

Look for Experience and Quality Time

This is why it takes more than one quick-sale conversation to come up with the right solution. I often require several meetings and take considerable detail into consideration about client lifestyles and finances before I can make the best decision. Only then can I begin to put together the right plan from the myriad of products and features in the annuity marketplace. I spent many years perfecting my uniquely proprietary discovery process, learning everything an advisor needs to know while assembling the very best products and features for my clients. And yet I STILL take the time - my own time, not yours - to *get it right* for you and your situation.

Be wary of anyone who claims, after your first meeting, to have "just the annuity for you." This is not possible. A true financial professional will spend a great deal of time getting to know you. Because they know the market so well, they will spend much less time digging through product lines. But it still takes time to *get it right*.

Probate Repellant

Estate planners consider a side-benefit of the annuity one of the more powerful attributes of this versatile instrument: *Annuities avoid probate.*

This quality, alone, has made the annuity one of the most favored of all financial instruments among beneficiary and legacy planners. All you have to do is check the consequences of leaving cash in a savings account, or a safe deposit box, or in bonds. If you want these assets to avoid probate a lawyer would probably have this to say: "Don't even think about it."

Avoid probate. You can do this with annuities. While your grandfather's annuities were basically one-trick ponies, modern annuities come with a large catalogue of custom features to enhance flexibility, withdrawal options and more including:

- **Guaranteed growth rates**

- **Lifetime time income *for one or both spouses!***

- **Built-in Death Benefits**

- **Protection from Costs Associated with Catastrophic Illness**

'Reset' Your Earnings Threshold

Resets determine how your earnings will be protected in fixed indexed annuities, also how your earnings will be calculated. This process is called the "Annual Reset."

A Fixed Indexed Annuity's annual reset will "lock in" your interest earnings each year. At this time, the value of a given index will be reset, which means that any future stock market *decrease will not affect the value* of interest you have already earned.

This is what protection from market volatility is all about and it can be found with insurance companies. If the market goes south, your annuity value would . . . not . . . be . . . touched!

Where else in the investment world can you find this kind of guarantee? Not many. In so-called "technical" terms, the increased value of an FIA account is seen by the addition, or increased numbers of, your "index credits." These appear on your statement at, or around, the stipulated annual "anniversary date" in the contract and they "credit" your account with a locked-in new value. Again, your "index credits" cannot be lost during a market crash.

At the same time, the addition of an index credit to the value of your account *adds to the new, bottom-line value* of your account. In other words, index credits create a higher new baseline of principal, upon which the potential earning of additional new index credits would be based. All of which are *continuously protected and guaranteed*, as you essentially re-enter the market in the new year as an *investment participant* with your insurance company, but with an accordingly higher level of earning potential based on the index credits you have accumulated in the past.

It's a beautiful thing to watch: As the market grows, you grow the value of your account. Your account will increase from the point of your last reset. If it sounds a bit like compounding interest, it works in much the same way, but your earnings would be based on *upside* activity in the market.

It's important to note that people who want steady, guaranteed, uninterrupted compounding should go with standard fixed annuities, and I can help with that. Some of the larger estates have so much money they simply want the best possible compounding instrument they can find, from the most reliable carrier. But many people today want the potential market participation a good, Fixed Indexed Annuity can offer, without risk to principal or prior index-credit earnings.

An Investor Ideal

Many an investor who suffered heavy market losses - and sleepless nights awaiting the next market drop - consider the Fixed Indexed Annuity an ideal position, a place in the market without risk. They know it means freedom from the ugly prospect of having to, first, recover previous losses just to reach zero (basis) . . . otherwise known as Sequence of Returns Risk.

The Fixed Indexed Annuity is, in the opinion of many to investment analysts, one of the best solutions for the prevention of SOR!

Income Riders: Welcome Aboard!

Let's talk a bit about income riders and Fixed Indexed Annuities.

If you want income, you want to attach what is known as either a "lifetime income rider" or a "lifetime income benefit rider" to your Fixed Indexed Annuity. The income rider is a stipulated feature attached in writing to the main body of an annuity contract. Variations abound but this is how you can give yourself a steady stream of income for life, without risking your retirement savings.

If you want lifetime income guarantees, carriers tend to offer this option before you buy an annuity. In other words, choose your income rider option and attach it to the annuity you want to buy. It works best this way for the carrier because it gives you a lifetime income-stream IN PLACE of receiving 'annuitized' payments from your annuity in the future. Your income thus becomes a schedule of withdrawals from the annuity. But here's the payoff: Most income riders still set a guaranteed amount of *growth* for the annuity. Growth is based on a guaranteed income percentage, multiplied by the value of your account, which is set according to your age at the time you decide to begin receiving payments from the annuity.

FIA Benefits . . .

- *Asset protection*

- *Growth*

- *Shield against market risk*

- *Locked-in gains*

- *Income you cannot outlive.*

The most important thing you can do *in retirement* is to change the way you once managed your money! You cannot do it the way you did it during your working years! Fixed Indexed Annuities provide a proven way of managing retirement savings and income for retirees today! What I'm saying is simply this:

- *It is high time for you to stop worrying about another round of disastrous market losses.*

- *Forget about old planning methods based on traditional pension plans*

- *Avoid relying on income based on stocks and bonds.*

- *Market technology has reduced the odds of winning for average investors*

- *New investment threats include things we never worried about in the past.*

Rules Have Changed

Times have changed. We're living longer than ever before. Even as many investors and their advisors cling to the past, new and exciting retirement planning tools are available *right now*. These advanced tools are ready to meet the challenge of a new era of retirement planning. We're learning new ways to look at retirement. We're discovering ways to enjoy life while trimming our lifestyles. We're learning to master our retirements according to income managed by risk-free assets including Fixed Income Annuities.

As far as those stuck in the past, you may ask your broker about the Fixed Indexed Annuity. If he has little to say, other than to urge you to "stay the course," you know what I have to say about that: "Run." If you are interested in Fixed Income Annuities, I've already done the legwork. I've spent thousands of hours on research.

I have decades of experience with clients who have achieved the maximum lifestyle possible through Fixed Indexed Annuities.

But I don't expect you to take my word for all of the above and, for that very reason, I'm about to introduce you to someone who has been there. He will show you how it works from the consumer point of view, and from the standpoint of someone who is "living the life"

He's also a former pastor who lost heavily in the crash. I was happy to help him save his well-deserved retirement lifestyle from extinction and he will tell you, in his own words, how living with joy and peace of mind is what really counts . . . knowing that he can have a worry-free lifestyle as long as he lives!

CHAPTER THIRTEEN

'Living the Life' with Certainty

WE'VE TAKEN A close look at Social Security and made an even closer examination of annuities and how they work. We've explored the extremities of a planning tool only now being better understood by the financial community at large. I'm so glad people from all parts of the financial services industry are finally leaning in for a closer look at guaranteed income. I also hope they'll do their homework and realize how multi-faceted this kind of retirement solution can truly be, also that it must become *the 'priority approach of the century' when it comes to retirement planning.*

The following illustration is my reality-TV version of "living the life" with one of my strategies. As you now know after reading this book, Fixed Income Annuities and Social Security can create a solid foundation for your retirement, which looks fine in theory. Now, let's look inside the lifestyle of an actual plan at work, through the eyes of an individual who, like many of you, lived through the "lost decade." He endured the impact of Sequence of Returns Risk and moved on to become one of my clients.

Like him, you have now seen the writing on the wall. You have had a chance to examine the numbers, the reasons behind the cycles, the predictive factors ahead. You have seen the historic chronology of past markets. You can easily see the coming hurdles: Taxation, Debt and Volatility from oil producing regions to overseas markets, among many. And Congress will soon respond to mounting pressure to balance our national debt, while the feds are predicted to finally address artificially low interest rates in the near future.

Rather than feel the tension and uncertainty among market investors, after you adopt my planning methods these issues will sound like "business as usual." You would have the carefree ability to simply shrug them off and go back to your gardening, or the beach, or your favorite fishing spot. I hope the following account will put you in just such a "moment," shedding light on much more than a bunch of numbers on a chart.

A Survivor's Time Machine

You are about to step into a "Survivors Time Machine." You'll know what I mean in a moment. As you do, know that his words are his own, not mine. If you have money in the market right now — as many do - I want you to put yourself in the "moment" and reflect very carefully on the story I am about to introduce. After reading his story, I will then pose a question.

When I saw him last - which was not long ago at all — Paul was still a pastor and enjoying a comfortable semi-retirement, at age 83, still serving and being very much a beloved part of his community in central Connecticut. In the aftermath of the Great Recession, Paul said, "We keep going - that's what we do!" And so he leads his interdenominational congregation. I help him with that, from time to time. But that is not what the story is about.

The value of Paul's story is his wisdom, his foresight and, yes, his kind of faith, which is more invaluable today than ever before. People are out there right now, clinging to a skyrocketing stock market, afraid to let go, lacking faith in a few simple, financial instruments that would save them from potentially hazardous things to come. This is why Paul's story is important.

I have given you all kinds of information and you could use that information right now. But, as I said near the beginning of this book, "I don't expect you to take my word for it." In other words, I've suggested the importance of getting a second opinion. Well, here's one second opinion. Again, his name is Paul:

****

"Dave Reindel and I met for the first time many years ago, when I had my money in different places. Years later, something was bothering me so I went to see Dave. I went in to see Dave, specifically, because I know Dave likes annuities, and I knew I could trust him. Before I was ordained and went into the ministry, I used to sell annuities myself, so I knew what annuities could do.

"When Dave and I met, neither of us knew our nation was on the brink of economic disaster. At the time, almost all of my money was in a mutual fund - all of which was in stock - and I wasn't comfortable. I wanted out, on the spot, and Dave was able to get me out. You may not believe the reason for the timing of that meeting, but *I believe* it.

"David Reindel got me and my money out of that mutual fund, out of the market altogether. Not only was Dave able to get me out of the mutual fund in time, he was able to put me into a plan that would allow me to keep all my money. He put all of my money into annuities.

"It wasn't much more than a week later that the market crashed."

"We had made the switch to annuities just before October, 2008! If we hadn't, I would have lost a bundle, yet I didn't lose anything. *The Lord kept telling me to get out.* The timing was perfect and I'm very grateful because *I was able to save everything.* I believe it was divine intervention, and I believe Dave Reindel was there for a purpose, *just in time.*

"My money is still in those annuities. I have my Social Security."

"Those are my sources of income today and *I'm just fine.*"

"As I said, before that day in 2008, everything I had I'd had in mutual funds, so a major part of our money would have been gone, overnight.

Instead, my wife and I have our annuities and we're collecting income right now. I started taking income from one of them when I was 79 and it will be good for many years to come. Another one of my annuities is called an Immediate Annuity, which began with the contribution of a single premium and the immediate payout of income. Dave put others together to cover different time periods, but the main message is this: *At my age, it's really nice to know I'll get the same amount of money every month.*

"Looking way back, when I was in my late 50s we had been heading into yet another recession – one of many - which is interesting because hard times would more than repeat themselves in 2008! Maybe I was getting concerned in early 2008 because of my age.

I'd looked at those free-dinner invitations from financial planners and went to five or six. Back then I'd hear a lot of people say, "Don't put your money into annuities: they'll take your money out of play in the stock market." Maybe that was why I'd been going to a financial advisor in town, who had told me to put all sorts of assets in the market. Anyway, that's the way things had been going until I connected with Dave.

"I'm glad I did, especially after October, 2008. David is doing a great service for his clients when he puts financial stability in their future. It was obviously a life-saver for us. My son-in-law had a big income before the crash. He had a lot of money in the stock market and he took a beating. Well, I didn't.

"I've felt very secure with our annuities and I still believe, with Dave's guidance, that it was a wise move on my part to get into the annuities I have now. When I try to talk to my kids about retirement, I certainly recommend that they have annuities in their portfolios. Both of their families have decent incomes. My older daughter and her husband are pretty savvy about looking into what they do with their money. But I think safety of principal and certainty about future income make all the difference when you get to my age.

"I tell my congregation to not be overly concerned about what's going on in the world, economically, because we're under God's economy. God said He would supply all our needs according to His riches and glory. The way I see it, our investment ideas were transformed in October, 2008, as part of God's promise. I think a lot of people have gotten hold of that, including myself. It's also not surprising that the person who helped saved our retirement would go on to help us in so many ways. Dave's money has immeasurably helped our church. He has given generously to our Paid In Full prison ministry, which helps released former-prisoners with food, clothing and a place to live. Dave isn't an active member of our church, but he keeps giving generously to the church, and to other places in the community.

"In fact, I think he has probably given back all the money I have ever given to him and I've never said a word to him about giving. We were talking business one evening in his office and he said, out of the blue, "Oh, here, before you go . . . " He handed me an envelope. Inside there was a $10,000 check for our ministries. When I saw the check I cried. What a blessing! The Bible says, "Give and it shall be given unto you." I'm sure this must be part of Dave's success.

"Dave's integrity and giving to the community leads to the kind of reputation he enjoys today. His financial planning service is important, too, because financial prosperity is, after all, part of God's will. Scriptural teachings about money and money management include *Deuteronomy 8:18*, which says, "God gives us the power to get wealth" so His covenant may be established. People need to understand that God must be involved in what they're doing financially.

"We are also charged with being (financially) vigilant and I think annuities play a role in that."

"On that note, while our October, 2008, investment in annuities saved us financially, I later . . . discovered that part of God's covenant is healing. I wish we'd known sooner: God wants his people to prosper. He wants his people to be healthy. After financially surviving the Crash of 2008 and the aftermath, the recession, I now think His will might also include financial health."

****

My thanks to Paul for his kind, and insightful, words. I couldn't agree more and, as promised, here's the question I have for you: Are you ready financially? Will your life savings be able to survive another economic apocalypse? If you are over 55, the slightest market correction could pose a real setback to your future. It could delay your long-awaited first day of retirement for many years.

I want you to imagine being on the very brink of the Crash of 2008, like Paul. If you knew then what you know NOW would you delay your retirement another second? Are you ready to roll over those Qualified Plans? Are you willing to have a little faith in something other than total market risk and maybe – just possibly – save your retirement?

Paul's story should be more than just a warning. It should be a wake-up call. You have the opportunity to cash-out of financial uncertainty and cash-in to a solid, reliable foundation of lifetime income . . . an untouchable cornerstone of monthly paychecks you could never outlive . . . no matter what happens when mayhem strikes world economies. And it will.

- **Maximize your Social Security benefit.**

- **Secure your savings in annuities.**

- **Guarantee yourself some income.**

- **Protect your principal.**

It's Your Money: Don't Risk It! Make it . . . Grow!

Amen. Let's move on to your legacy.

CHAPTER FOURTEEN

Guaranteed Legacy Solutions

ONE OF THE potential pitfalls of inadequate financial planning is the lack of protection for a family legacy. I'm not sure what goes on in the minds of some people as they look at everything else on the horizon – everything but the state of their own affairs, financial assets and valuable property after they die.

You wouldn't give away an ancestor's ruby broche to just anyone walking down the street, especially if it has been in your family for generations. Yet, I've seen post-mortem estates left in a shambles of poor management, with scattered versions of undated wills lying in the same drawer with life insurance policies lacking a named beneficiary – or at least a living beneficiary. I've seen valuable classic cars go to auction due to a lack of documentation, with proceeds held up in probate or, worse, as proceeds released to 'outlaw in-laws.'

It can be especially disarming to see the equity in a beloved family home seized by the court to pay for probate costs. But these things happen all the time, according to different laws in different states. You need to have an Elder Law attorney look into legal protections in force, to ensure that your belongings and financial assets go to the proper heirs. Don't just expect that "somebody in the family will handle everything."

Organize . . . to Preserve and Protect

Without taking proper steps to protect your entire legacy, any number of things can happen to almost everything you own. The following cover some of the essentials of your "Legacy Check List:"

- Have you made the decision to gather up all of your important documents and file them in one, safe place, in a clearly organized manner? I'm not saying that *you* don't know exactly where they are as you read this, but what if something happens to you immediately after you put down this book? Would your spouse or loved ones know where to look for your estate-preservation documents? Having an easy to follow and up-to-date *filing system* for your financial and legal documents is not only for your own peace of mind, it's really for those who would be dealing with, say, doctors, hospitals and health insurance carriers – if you were suddenly incapacitated and temporarily unable to handle your own affairs.

While everyone in America should have readily accessible, signed and updated *medical power of attorney* forms in the house - maybe even *living will* documents in the same location - every retiree *absolutely* must have such things in easy reach. Not only in place and well-filed, but with some sort of notification of their whereabouts posted nearby – say, above a desk in a den beside your "All Documents" filing cabinet. Otherwise, the outcome of sudden illness – one small example - could escalate into a real, financial and emotional catastrophe – both for you and for the loved ones in charge of your affairs.

- Moving on, let's assume you got in touch with us and we were able to put your documents in order – as we tidy up your affairs in other areas. *Have you taken steps to make sure all appropriate instruments have their beneficiary forms attached?* This is critically important.
- Have you made sure that your beneficiary forms have *beneficiaries accurately, and properly noted?* If this hasn't been done, or hasn't been done in a while, *I can help.*

- Here's one many people overlook: While we make sure that our designated beneficiaries are named on the proper forms, and that the proper forms are in their proper places, people often forget to *name contingency beneficiaries* on these forms, which can lead to a number of unpleasant consequences. I won't go into detail here, but what if a $500,000 Death Benefit is to go to a *deceased* beneficiary? Where do you think all that money will go? I have the answers, which can be both surprising and alarming. *A lack of updated beneficiary forms can create havoc for your legacy.*
- Are you aware of what happens to your Social Security benefits if you die? Has your spouse been made aware of what to expect, and what to do? A spouse has the right to claim the greater of two benefits after the death of the other spouse, among other possibilities. Again, I can help you with solutions, which you should keep in your documents file.
- Here's the BIG one: Have you carefully organized all of your *estate planning documents*? We could be talking about anything from insurance policies and annuity contracts to real estate deeds and other legal instruments?
- Some of your estate-planning documents would include the potential ability to provide *multi-generational payouts* to your heirs, which would make a difference in their lives, and in the lives of their loved ones for generation-upon-generation to come. For questions of this nature, get in touch with me right away.

Beneficiaries Take Precedence over All Others

Above all other documents and in order of importance, *the beneficiary form takes precedence over Wills, Trusts and Divorce documents.* I work in a world of beneficiary forms. I know what must be done. I know how to help you update beneficiaries and the instruments that would provide their benefits.

When it comes to your estate and the literal "state" of your affairs, how do our money strategies come to play in this area? If your insurance policies and brokerage accounts are heaped into one file drawer, while bank statements are piled in a closet with records of your CDs – here I apply the color "red." This means "stop" everything and look carefully for every document you can find. Go out to Target and buy a filing cabinet or safe if you must. Store everything in one place. Leave a posted list of items in your files, and directions as to where to find them – leave this list in the top drawer of your desk at home, at your office and with one or two of your closest friends or loved ones. Then it's time for the color "yellow," pointing to the need to "pay attention" to new insurance addendums and other documents, carefully filing each one as it comes to your door. That done, your "green" files are those that have been fully resolved, with no further action needed; you might want to have my advice, and the advice of your attorney, before putting documents in this file.

Now you can go on with the rest of your life, knowing that your estate will be in order when it really counts.

Strategic Allocation

So, you've taken my advice and secured all documentation in its proper place, where others can find it during emotionally and financially stressful times. Good. But have you forgotten the most important thing? This "thing" could make or break the financial outcome of your estate, forever, leaving your heirs in, or free of, emotional upheaval?

Here's The Thing: the proper *allocation* of your *assets* for ultimate protection of your estate. Failing to allocate your assets properly will:

- **Leave your property vulnerable to probate**

- **Put your financial assets in the path of attack from market risk**

- **Open the doors to court challenges by outsiders**

- **Set family members against one another after you die**

When we talk about protecting a family estate and multi-generational family legacy, who in the world should we really trust? Some rely on bankers, other on a lawyer, and still others leave everything to a financial planner of one kind or another. If you intend to trust someone with your entire financial life, all I can say is that you had better do your homework. The world is full of:

- *Dubious banking products and promotions*

- *Financial scams of all kinds*

- *Financial advice freely given by people who only recently were selling sofas and refrigerators – are they equipped to give you "good" advice?*

Beneficiary-Planning Essentials

Here's a final word and more specifics about *"beneficiary planning"* and, again, please call my office anytime for help with this important matter. I'm so adamant about beneficiary management and planning when it comes to estate preservation, it tends to be one of the first items on my agenda when I meet with people in retirement.

While I've already noted that beneficiary forms trump everything else in estate planning – from wills to divorce decrees – certain signed documents might lead you to believe otherwise. Don't believe it. *Failing to routinely review beneficiary forms could be the biggest mistake of your life.* I say this from decades of planning experience. You now know to update your beneficiary forms and put them in a safe place easily located by others – people you can trust, of course. You also know to put in writing on your forms both primary and contingent beneficiaries . . .

But *do your forms allow for the "restriction" of a beneficiary?* Do they address the needs of minor children as beneficiaries, and do your beneficiary forms even *allow* a multi-generational payout? Aha! If not, come see me.

Let's talk about your designated beneficiaries in the realm of maximizing IRA and 401k accounts. Now, if you are in retirement, let's get back to a fundamental question: Why would you still be IN those old, Qualified Contribution Plans? Give me a call and let me send you a free report explaining the importance of the classic Rule of 100. When you call us at 800.639.5113, please ask me, or anyone on my staff, to give you the "Rule of 100 Report," specifically. It will more fully detail the reason for proper allocation strategies as we age.

That said, if you are in an IRA or 401K – for whatever reason – you should be aware of at least a few basics: Did you know that *transfers of inherited IRAs to non-spousal beneficiaries must be on a **trustee-to-trustee** basis*? It's true. If your intended IRA beneficiary is not going to be your spouse, *the Non-Spousal IRA Beneficiary may not become the new owner of an inherited IRA.*

- This individual ***cannot roll the inherited IRA into THEIR OWN IRA!***

- Non-Spousal Beneficiaries are ***not allowed a 60-day rollover period***!

- And **Non-Spousal Beneficiary IRA assets become an IMMEDIATELY TAXABLE distribution!**

We've all heard the stories from friends, or friends of friends: After Grandpa passed away, somebody – a grandchild, nephew, whomever - was all excited about being named as Grandpa's IRA beneficiary . . . until he/she found out that the government was going to take out a huge chunk for taxes. Let's face it, this can become an infuriating experience for heirs, especially when they get the money, rush out and spend the money, then get hit with a "huge" – and often unpayable – tax bill at a later time.

Ultimate IRA Solutions vs. Upsetting Outcomes

A very simple solution involves the creation of a "Direct Rollover" mechanism allowing Grandpa's IRA to rollover from ***trustee-to-trustee.***

This is a most important advantage for heirs. This method allows them to:

- *Avoid the "20% mandatory-withholding" AND the 60-day Rule (call me, I'll explain)*

- *Continue to GROW THE MONEY tax-deferred*

- *Control where the IRA money is invested while providing more investment options*

- *Maintain the Multi-Generational Option*

- *Maintain the Roth Conversion Option*

I can't say enough about the importance of advanced-planning IRA strategies when it comes to beneficiaries. Planning is the only way to keep heirs from losing big chunks of their IRA inheritance to the tax man. *If you would like to learn more about how to properly rollover your 401(k), 403(b), 457, TSP – or any other IRA retirement account . . . call me.*

For you, a properly implemented IRA rollover strategy might sound like a precarious and mind-numbing process. Not for me. I do this every day. I do it because more and more people realize how important it is to put an IRA rollover strategy in motion. Please do not leave this to one of many potential loved ones; they may be vulnerable to predatory influences in the financial world today.

Vulnerable Loved Ones

One of the greatest potential pitfalls in estate-legacy planning is to leave a less-than-savvy loved one vulnerable to the wrong kinds of advice. After you pass away, all sorts of vultures will try to descend on your children and/or grandchildren, your home, your assets and other properties. Leave a stamp collection to a 12-year-old grandson and he's off to the nearest 'coin' shop, hoping to cash in: What kind of advice will he get? Will the shopkeeper act in your grandson's best interest?

What about the spouse you leave behind? Will he or she be enticed to free luncheons with all sorts of financial schemes attached? Have you really made an effort to provide, on behalf of your loved ones, an advisor you know and trust? If you haven't, it's about time to do just that.

Understand Your Sources

You need to understand the source of advice you take to heart. When I talk about the "source" of someone's foundational advisory powers, it usually comes from a certain orientation.

With some advisors, this orientation goes deep, spanning decades into the past. With others, the source of advice comes from a few weeks, or months, in some 'boot-camp' training program designed to push certain financial products . . . not exactly a well-spring "source," but some people are very gifted at selling, even if they're not sure of the long-range outcome for their customers.

I'm still amazed that more people haven't jumped on the band-wagon when embracing key issues in upcoming chapters. The next chapter hopefully puts more of a face on what can happen in the absence of effective legacy planning.

CHAPTER FIFTEEN

Nightmares on Main Street . . . Avoiding Inheritance Horrors

W E'VE ADDRESSED THE consequences of leaving your assets to probate, among other issues, but we haven't talked about inheritance issues and the sometimes devastating conflicts that may arise among surviving friends and family members.

With skillful legacy planning aboard from the beginning, you can rest easy, knowing that your assets would go to intended recipients. Why would you need a skillful legacy planner in your corner? Why not just write up your own 'online-easy-will' and let the chips fall where they may? The following represent more than a few reasons why proper wills, trusts and beneficiary stipulations should be considered a must-have for your legacy plan:

After you have "left the building" so to speak, leaving assets in the hands of your children could present real problems. It might sound a bit brutal, but let's imagine for a moment that you don't know who your children really are when it comes to handling money . . . until the time comes to divide an inheritance. I'm not talking about multi-billionaire dynasties, either. We've all heard about celebrity conflicts in this arena. Entire books have covered battles having to do with the estate of Elvis Presley and notorious contests over assets left behind by Howard Hughes.

How do we address the handling of inherited assets left behind for a financially immature child? Nice guy, sure, but after you gave him that

$10,000 gift a few years ago, he went straight to Vegas. This individual may be in his or her adult years but a spendthrift. In fact, you have probably heard about so-called "spendthrift trusts" in which assets are doled out over a long period of time. Your 'family gambler' might be a candidate for such a trust. . . . And what about his daughter, your beloved grandchild? Suppose you want to make sure a grandchild has a savings plan in place for college, many years down the road. Would you simply trust an adult child to save your bequest for your grandchild, without dipping into principal?

You should know that *I have instruments on hand that are tailor-made to deal with these situations* - with diplomacy, clarity and, *ultimate asset protection for all concerned*.

Putting it another way, would you risk seeing money earmarked for a grandchild's college tuition turn into a shopping spree at Saks Fifth Avenue for her mother? I know: these are sensitive issues. Try to discuss this in a "casual" family gathering and . . . well, look out!

You and I can discuss it privately, without family pressure, in a businesslike atmosphere where your feelings and wishes will be heard. This can be of particular importance if you have a disabled child in the family with special needs; a program could be set up to ensure that a flow of untouchable assets would be there for this special child, long after you are gone. Disabled people also need protection from predatory health care and other service providers, making advanced legacy planning absolutely necessary.

Legacies and Lingering Debt

You may be certain of a harmonious outcome among your family members, after inheritance issues are settled, and distributions have been made. But what about possible debt or delinquent credit card charges an adult child may not want to discuss with you? What would happen to her inheritance if creditors descended on her inheritance the moment the money goes into her bank account?

I can help you explore different ways to protect your legacy from your child's creditors. You can choose – right now – whether or not you want them to have a future stream of income or future college tuition for, say, a granddaughter – or let it go to one of their creditors.

Avoiding Conflict

Avoidance of conflict is at the heart of the matter when it comes to protecting loved ones after you are gone. Leave nothing to chance, or challenge, when it comes to properly drawn wills, trusts and, above all, the right kinds of instruments that designate, and protect, your chosen beneficiaries. You may have enough to worry about regarding conflict due to an unequal inheritance. Even when we know we've treated our children fairly with equal distribution of asset value, *they* may not see it that way. Power struggles ignite in an emotional atmosphere, especially when money is on the table.

We've all heard of estates left to one or two siblings, whom the deceased expected to be fair and distribute assets equally among other siblings. You might trust the "responsible" child with all your heart, but you may not know what would happen when valuable assets enter the picture. My suggestion is to first look at the child who had difficulty sharing in grammar school and expect something similar – however muted by diplomacy – among your adult survivors. I would also expect my own perceptions to be colored by - let's face it - a degree of favoritism.

After all is said and still undone, I would probably look for ways to designate each child as a named *beneficiary* of specific assets. Again, this is where I come in.

Property Perils

Leaving inherited property to the management of several siblings can be trouble – especially when it involves real estate and specifically rental property, or a second home. One sibling might feel put-upon by an overabundance of maintenance tasks, while other siblings bicker over who gets to use, and when, that inherited lakeside cabin.

I have several, highly qualified resources available to handle these situations, which might include an Elder Law attorney or some other professional. Let's talk it out. Every situation is different. Just know that I've seen and heard almost everything when it comes to the dissolution of estates, distribution of legacies, making sure that beneficiaries are properly named, and that assets have been appropriately passed along to future generations. This is part of what I do.

Inheritance Tactics

As we talk about securing your assets in the right kinds of instruments, this is probably the time to start asking questions about how much inheritance should go where, or to whom. Should you leave assets in a large lump sum? How much is too much inheritance at one time? Should you spread out an inheritance over a period of time? Perhaps you have considered periodic gifting while you are still alive – maybe not a bad idea, since you can actually watch how your beneficiaries spend what they get. Would you want a grandchild to immediately become a trust-fund- dependent after you die, or would you add stipulations – like finishing college?

Power Plays

I can't help you with the emotional mayhem of family power-plays, people suing other people because someone was cut out of a will. That's where a good estate-planning attorney comes in. But I *can* help you find the right kinds of guaranteed tools, backed by some of the world's most powerful institutions. These tools can ensure that *your* money will go where *you* want it to go, in such a way that a loved one would receive not only an income stream, but earnings to perpetuate that income stream.

It may be necessary to establish trustees to oversee an inheritance meant for an underage beneficiary, but you don't have to leave a cash-account in the hands of this trustee. You shouldn't, in my opinion. You can, however, leave the money in an instrument designated for distribution at some point in time, which can be monitored by a trustee.

In other words, I have all sorts of options at my fingertips to help you manage the future of your assets, *after* you die. This is what "legacy planning" is all about and insurance products are some of the very best ways to do the job. You can preserve and grow money for your heirs. You can provide assets for the care of minor children or grandchildren. You will discover many different options at your fingertips when we get together. Just do it before your affairs are unexpectedly left to someone else.

Alternative Legacies

You should look at how – if you were still alive - you would handle the distribution of your non-cash assets.

Perhaps some of these items could be liquidated and turned into ever-increasing earnings designed to grow at a fixed rate, over a long period of time. Maybe you have a beloved classic car in the garage, but how much do your heirs "love" the car? Would they simply put it on the auction block after the funeral? I'd find out.

Imagine taking the cash proceeds from the car – artwork, antiques, a valuable stamp collection – and turning the liquidated value into something that could grow to ten times current value, providing an income at a moment in time when your heirs would need it most. It could provide a lump sum for the down-payment on a first home, or a wedding, or private school tuition for grandchildren, or, ironically, a collectible car as a legacy-graduation present for a grandchild finishing college paid for by the legacy. The value of the legacy account would have grown far beyond the value of the original classic car in your garage today.

When you really think about it, how many families wind up wrangling over household contents after a second spouse passes away, or after a surviving spouse enters a nursing home? Human beings being human . . . will surviving family members race to Dad's house after the funeral to be the first ones on the scene - hoping to grab anything that isn't nailed down? Well, yes, they might – not saying *your* family members are like that . . . but wouldn't it make sense to liquidate valuable property and put it into something that would leave a lasting tribute to you? Let them quibble over a chipped set of dishes. Leave them a legacy of income and more.

Business Legacies

Lawyers and other specialists handle most issues surrounding business succession, but I may be able to help you create special legacies for key employees, maybe family members who have worked in the business, or simply those who may be out of a job should the business change hands after you die. And have you thought of how your business-owned properties would be liquidated? Leaving anything including your family home to probate could mean leaving equity exposed to probate costs. Perhaps the property could be placed in a trust then liquidated inside the trust after you are gone - with proceeds going into certain instruments providing an income stream for beneficiaries.

Options are many but what I'm really saying is this: When you arrange for the liquidation of a piece of property for re-investment, and a later, evenly balanced, distribution among surviving family members, you take emotional attachment to that property out of the situation, protecting your wishes and feelings among family members at the same time. Family real estate holdings can be handled in a myriad of different ways, of course, calling for an altogether different set of professionals. All I want you to do is think ahead, then plan ahead. I can help you sort things out and assemble the right plan of action . . . while you still have something to say about it!

This brings up one particularly sensitive issue, and it happens too often these days: Let's say a family patriarch is in his second or third marriage. He dies, leaving "everything" to the second or third spouse, meaning the husband basically dumps a hornet's nest of issues into the lap of someone not exactly blood-related to surviving children and grandchildren.

- ***Will his surviving spouse leave "everything" to his children or grandchildren?***

- *Will she leave everything to someone else, someone he never knew in his own life, like a new husband?*

- *Will she choose to leave his assets to her tennis pro or golf teacher?*

- *Will the children of the second spouse battle children of the first?*

- *By now you should know better than to leave it to a "Will" and probate!*

I don't have to remind anyone of the horror stories in this potentially contentious area. This is the very kind of emotional atmosphere destined to explode. Is it right to just dump everything in the account of a surviving spouse – at a time when families should come together in mutual support?

Annuities to the Rescue

Perhaps you could set aside assets for your heirs that would provide for each of them, *no matter what happens.* If the family patriarch in this illustration were to establish an annuity for each of his children, or grandchildren, it would be able to grow and compound. It could be put into an index-related annuity with the potential to 'explode' in a positive way, gaining untold value for the future of the beneficiary. You could add a Death Benefit. You could add all sorts of features. Rather than leave it all to the fortunes of probate, wills, attorneys fighting other attorneys, or potentially hostile family members, you could defuse the situation in a way that would guarantee benefits for everyone.

I say this because in estates involving multiple spouses and multiple families, more than enough issues must be left to attorneys. I am not an attorney, but I have to wonder what happens when a parent in a second marriage dies. Who gets his or her half of the estate, kids from the first marriage or kids who came into the marriage with the new spouse? Do I know what will happen. No way. Do you? Can anyone say with absolute certainty that a second spouse would "do the right thing," and distribute assets equally? No.

Protect a Surviving Spouse

Now let's look at a surviving spouse. Will he or she be protected after you die, particularly if you die prematurely? I'm now talking about the possibility of children, even grandchildren, aggressively attempting to take control of assets . . . while the surviving spouse is *still alive*. If you leave money lying around in a savings account, persuasive family members can become predatory family members, leaving an elderly spouse in financial straits.

Have you considered leaving assets for your spouse in the form of a lifetime income stream that can never be challenged, or lost to market risk? I've been talking about protecting retirement lifestyles from risk with annuities all along. Now I'm talking about protecting an elderly spouse from relatives who would use her savings to invest in (pick one): a "bargain" property, "hot stock," a large sum of money for a grandchild's private school tuition . . . enough to leave your surviving spouse struggling to make ends meet.

If You Become Incapacitated

We haven't really addressed the fate of retirement assets when a surviving spouse becomes incapacitated, or incompetent. I hate to say it but I've seen children become as devious as perfect strangers when it comes to assets exposed by a spouse's medical situation. I guess the real question is whether an elderly person actually wants to be left in charge of vulnerable assets.

If you are in your mid-80s or early 90s, do you want to have all sorts of loose financial strings lying around in CDs, savings accounts, checking accounts, or jewelry in a jewelry box? Would it be better for a surviving spouse to have everything neatly bundled into a guaranteed income stream safe from probate, family members, creditors, and predators with dubious investment schemes?

I can definitely help in this situation. Please, before it's too late, give me a call and we can make sure that everyone of your surviving loved ones will be protected. I can do this with reliable, dependable financial instruments backed by some of the most powerful companies in America. These companies have top scores from ratings services like Morningstar to A.M. Best.

Grandchildren, Taxes and Your Legacy

You can provide for grandchildren who may never get the financial help they need unless you step in. You can set up a financial program that would be there for them, no matter what happens. With a timeline of many years, assets within this program could grow into a comparative fortune when they come of age. You can always leave behind an inheritance for grandchildren, of course, but how safe would the money be if the assets were prevented from growing? What if they were left at risk or siphoned off by financial predators?

Taxing Your Legacy

Have you considered the impact of "death taxes" on your legacy? Have you considered options that could greatly mitigate the tax before it turns into income for your heirs?

As designated beneficiaries in certain instruments, an inheritance can live on as an income stream while being allowed to compound and grow at the same time. In other words, yes, the IRS must be informed when assets go to heirs, but as we've already seen, the manner in which the assets are transferred can mean the difference between the significant preservation – or considerable loss – of someone's inheritance.

Rather than accept the "death tax" consequence as-is – as it would apply to a lump-sum inheritance – we could look at ways of transferring your wealth while avoiding excessive taxation. Not only do you have the option to reduce the tax bite for your heirs, you can protect them with a distribution schedule further protecting them from predators.

It all comes down to what you want to do. If you feel patriotic and want to leave an oversized chunk of your child's inheritance to the IRS, go ahead. This would be patriotic, indeed, because the heavily taxed money you left to a child could be taxed *again* when your child dies.

Otherwise, you can choose to legally, responsibly and ethically leave more money to your children, grandchildren, other heirs or favorite charities.

And while we're on the subject of heirs and governments, we have covered the topic of Social Security as it applies to you and your benefits. We've touched upon Spousal Benefits and extending the moment you take your benefits. But have you considered what happens to the Social Security benefit of an heir who receives a financial windfall from inheritance? It can be an issue. If inheritance is handled the wrong way, a child can be disqualified for receiving the SSI benefits he or she deserves!

If you are a potential heir as well as a Social Security benefit recipient, you want to get in touch with me. I have strategies in mind that could help you keep the entitlements you have coming to you, while protecting your inheritance from other threats – like taxation discussed above. If you know of someone who needs advice in this important area of retirement planning, I can offer some objective, third-party assistance.

"New Friends . . . "

An unattended inheritance can quickly evaporate without proper planning and tools specifically designed to transfer wealth, while protecting assets. Potential heirs and beneficiaries might consider these unforeseen hurdles *before* they wind up with grandpa's money. In other words, have you discussed a plan to protect yourself and your beneficiaries?

When someone receives the "big inheritance," the hands come out, palms-up. A beneficiary may find herself with a sudden "wealth" of wanna-be business partners, and persuasive "new friends." This is where the young heir is talked into buying a share of some desert island, or a share in that enticing beachfront property with a view . . . and an approaching bust in the local real estate market.

Or, an adult child inherits your home, only to discover that a hefty, IRS "death tax" may apply to the transfer of ownership. A mishandled title transfer could even trigger the "death tax" as you live and breathe. You could be taxed on the transfer of your own home before you die! A number of strategies can be put into motion by appropriate professionals to reduce or even eliminate taxation, but you need to start asking questions now. You need to have an experienced financial professional in your camp who can direct you to the right people (that would be me).

I am all about preserving assets and securing income. I have a passion for helping people save money in any way possible, right down to the last protectable penny of your Social Security benefit. If I have a passion for that, don't you think I would do everything possible to make sure your legacy would be protected as well? You bet I will!

Before potential heirs find themselves in any of the situations above, it would behoove their benefactor (you) to protect them in advance. Act now and you can make sure that their inheritance will continue to grow and compound, rather than blow away in the next breeze of momentary temptation. Act now and you could ensure that their inheritance money would be available as they reach an age when a lifetime stream of retirement income sounds infinitely more valuable than having a speed boat!

You might ask, "Why not let them make up their own minds about what to do with my money?" You might see your kids as pillars of common sense and investment savvy, but think back to the days when 'old age' was a distant concept left to 'old people.' You had your whole life ahead of you. Things like retirement income didn't seem as important as they eventually, inevitably would. Even the most astute young investors can be tempted to blow money on "sure thing" opportunities on Wall Street. Face it, we've all been there. But as you near retirement, priorities change. All of a sudden you find yourself doing everything possible to cobble together enough monthly income for a decent retirement lifestyle.

A Legacy of Guaranteed Income

Wouldn't it be nice if your kids could have the advantage of an income waiting-to-happen, when they're old enough to appreciate its value? Family legacies have been based on just such an idea.

Family assets have been passed from generation to generation, not only maintaining wealth and secure lifestyles, but to actually *perpetuate* the family legacy! Do you know how to make sure that your inheritance instructions would be respected, let alone implemented after you die? Ask yourself the tough questions: "Do I really know my kids? Can I be absolutely guaranteed that they would follow my legacy plan to the letter, after I'm gone?"

You have already seen what can happen to stipulations in wills. You know what happens to property left to probate, which is sometimes unavoidable, but you also have options that would allow your heirs to bypass probate altogether. You know what I'm talking about. I have been working with different types of annuities, for so long, I have been able to find just the right products to work in almost every kind of situation.

You need a lawyer to tell you why it might not be a great idea to share Joint Tenancy with one of your kids. However, you will need an annuity specialist to show how to pass assets to the next generation with minimal impact, maximized earnings, guaranteed principal and future income. I'm saying that your lawyer can write up a proper "Living Trust," which can protect your assets from probate.

I can structure assets in a way that would automatically by-pass probate altogether.

Again, it's all about you. I can stand at a lectern all day and talk to an audience until I drop from exhaustion. But I cannot make anyone get out of his chair and make the next move. I hope I've been able to put everything in a proper light for your situation. More than anything, I hope you can see new possibilities for yourself and for your future.

I also hope I have taken your vision one last step, providing a better picture of what your hard-earned lifetime savings can do for people you know and love – not some predator, creditor or government agency.

Will a "Will" Work for You?

Remember that a "will" is just that, an expression of your will. It's a legal document intended to name, on your behalf, the heirs and charities you have chosen to receive your assets after you die. A will is subject to probate. All property left in a will is subject to probate. Probate is simply a method used to disburse property. Probate decisions can be made by a probate judge and, all told, this process can take a very long time, as expenses mount for your loved ones.

A *Living Trust* differs from a will in that you can put property into your Living Trust, while acting as your own trustor or trustee. In your Living Trust, you can name beneficiaries and a succeeding trustee when you die, who would then distribute property and assets from your estate according to your written wishes. Although many benefits can be had with a properly drafted Living Trust, the best by far is that *a well-drafted Living Trust avoids probate*.

Proceeds from an annuity also avoid probate, if they have been left to a beneficiary other than an estate. The same applies to life insurance policy pay-outs, as well as property left to a surviving spouse.

Unfortunately, *a will cannot avoid probate*. It is an instrument used in the probate process. *The existence of a will may, in fact, trigger probate*, which is why you should *consider annuities and other means to avoid it*. Your life in retirement may be challenging enough without having to worry about your legacy being challenged in probate.

Now you know what to do. Let's talk.

****

This is an ideal moment to break from the discussion above to one of the more quickly emerging trends in the financial world today. The trend has been gaining the attention of personal finance blogs, radio shows and publications, also retirement journals and retirement associations.

I'm talking about the new and commanding role women have taken, and will continue to take, in the financial world – especially as *boomer women* take on mountains of inherited assets from their parents . . . and from their deceased husbands. Often unexpected challenges await women who left financial matters to their spouses, especially if these women are left without guidance in the sometimes treacherous process of wealth transfer.

Men should take note of the following chapter as well: The women in your lives should have all the knowledge and ability possible to counter adverse influences, particularly before you die. At such times, emotions mingled with chaotic planning could leave your assets vulnerable to financial turmoil and predators with schemes designed to access your hard-earned financial legacy.

CHAPTER SIXTEEN

Eradicating Financial Uncertainty
... Women Take Charge

I DON'T CARE ABOUT shouting headlines. Nor do I don't pay much attention to "panic-news" on financial news channels because I don't deal in 'panic.' I'm in the business of de-fusing financial uncertainty. My clients don't panic, financially speaking, but the outside noise continues . . .

Internet web-logs (blogs) are even more troublesome, especially when it comes to following a financial guru on the internet because you often get no information about the writer's affiliations: He or she may have great credentials, but if he's on the payroll of certain, shall we say, "influences," you're going to get what they want to push. Some of the most highly experienced advisors accordingly come from an orientation cemented almost entirely to risk, even when they deal with people well into their retirement years.

After you pass away, this type of advisor could leave your beloved spouse financially stranded in the event of a market crash. An advisor might have made a career of selling mutual funds, dismissing things like Social Security as he urges your surviving spouse to adopt a laddered "diversity" of funds, which have various levels of "risk" tolerance – all at risk, of course.

Women Take Charge

More and more women will eventually step up to take charge of their family assets, estates and legacies. Let's face it: they will most likely take on the assets of a deceased spouse because – as noted earlier in this book - women generally outlive men. Women often wind up with the sum-total of all assets in a marriage after the death of a spouse . . . or after a divorce. Women have thus attracted increasing scrutiny from financial people selling all sorts of investment angles.

People in the financial world are aware more than ever that women will control an enormous mass of assets. In fact, women should be aware that some in the financial industry actually train to understand the female psyche. Conversely, women should be acutely aware of an advisor's orientation. I advise every woman to check out the background of advisors they intend to work with. When asking this individual for background information, if you don't get a prompt, clear, easily understood answer – both verbally, and in writing – I suggest that you head for the door.

The Five Financial Pitfalls of Financial Planning for Women include:

- **Not understanding the "source" of advice**

- **Failing to allocate assets appropriate to risk tolerance**

- **Misunderstanding, and failing to prepare for, legacy planning**

- **Failing to fill (or preparing to re-fill) the Income Gap**

- **Failing to get a second opinion**

Empowering Women in a New Millennium

The next little hurdle is to understand an advisor's role in the "risk" and "non-risk" categories of financial planning. I hope this book has given you a clear picture of the "non-risk" contingent. You will find a number of us and our numbers are growing by the day as people become aware of the wages of risk. You will also find many levels of ability in the "risk" advisor's world, although differences from one brokerage house to the next may vary considerably. Either way, when meeting with anyone about to handle your money, ask for his or her company's average client loss-and-gain average from October, 2008, through 2009. Conservative brokerage firms would probably give you an immediate answer, showing client losses considerably less than the widely quoted 50% drop in average portfolios. Again, if you can't get a straight answer after your first five minutes in the office, you know how to show yourself out.

That's the point. I'm always eager to show that my clients have never lost a dime.

If you happen to be a woman over 55 and near retirement, you already know how I feel: You should be working with an advisor who knows the ropes of safety, security, income *guarantees*, and the ultimate in asset *preservation* – NOT speculation. If an advisor wants to help you *dabble* in market investments, ask him where he puts his own assets. If you can't get a straight answer, I wouldn't be surprised if a sizeable amount of his money was in a life insurance product or annuity. Veteran brokers know *precisely why* major stock-and-bond investors were able to *clean up* on Wall Street after the Crash of 1929 while others jumped out of skyscrapers. Back then, just before the Crash of '29 (and before the 2008 meltdown), boatloads of smart-money had been placed in annuities and cash-value life insurance.

This gave the policy holder not only income guarantees but access to guaranteed principal, which was used to scoop up post-crash stocks and bonds for pennies on the dollar. Would you have given yourself, and your family, income guarantees if you knew that the rest of the financial world was about to lose everything? Of course, you would. The way women plan their legacies today will have the same, lasting effect on the future of this nation. That's my opinion. In the historic past, too many women left everything to men in the family when it came to money. They were often left with less than what they had coming as a result. Today, more and more women know that, as a surviving spouse, they may be left holding the bag when it comes to neglected tax issues and other perils, including important assets that were never properly transferred out of the husband's name. These include bank accounts without 'Paid-On-Death' or joint signatory status, insurance policies lacking beneficiary designations, and the list goes on. Fortunes have been lost accordingly in the intimidating turmoil of probate.

A Commanding Presence in the Financial Universe

Women have a more commanding presence in the workplace these days, stepping into high-ranking positions in powerful companies by leaps and bounds. Although "glass-ceiling" issues certainly persist, women have an increasing presence in the investment world as well, and in the retirement planning process.

More and more women are financially independent, self-employed and – if married – typically more interested in retirement planning for both spouses, more so than their male counterparts.

I have two women clients who exemplify the trend. One founded and ran her own company like a Swiss watch until the highly profitable family enterprise was sold. It was the woman who decided when to pull the plug and sell. It was the woman who got busy with retirement planning related to the sale. In the end, it was she who pulled together an array of somewhat disconnected resources and – after the sale of the business – put together a worry-free retirement for both herself and her husband, with enough guaranteed income for a nice lifestyle in retirement.

The second individual brought the remaining assets of her deceased former spouse's shaky investments into a new marriage. She then grew those assets until, one day, she found herself facing tough choices. Her second husband had just died. He had been a government pensioner and she saw his pension reduced when he died, so she met with me before the recession hit hard because she'd been reading business stories, tracking the way things were going in this country at the time. Together we pulled it all together and created a comfortable, dependable, independent lifestyle in retirement . . . just in time, by the way.

Women Take Charge

Women save more. They count pennies. They tend to scrutinize everything from both an interpersonal point of view – per a potential advisor – and from a money-practical point of view. I have many women as clients with similar stories. Some are single, some are widowed or divorced, some are married . . . and, as I said before, notably handling significant portions of the retirement planning process on behalf of both spouses. Women also tend to dive more thoroughly into the process, with more commitment and discipline than some men. They tend to put a lot of thought and care into their investments. They lean toward more reliable results, which almost invariably includes income guarantees and guaranteed safety of principle – while some of their male counterparts remain stubbornly entrenched in risk until it's too late.

Women vs. Risk

Women favor safety over risk, pure and simple. Many have become more confident since the crash when it comes to demanding safety of principal and long-term income guarantees. A good many women make important financial decisions more readily when compared to women of generations past. I see this on a regular basis as women seek my advice about the growing catalogue of features and functions of annuities. I can also safely say that my female clients will scrutinize a financial professional more closely than a lot of men. Same goes with my background: They understand the value of my lengthy background in the insurance industry. They respect my affiliations with appropriately degreed professionals in related fields. They look for higher levels of professionalism, making it helpful for me to show them my Registered Investment Advisor licensing, along with other certifications from the insurance industry *and* an academic background in mathematics.

At the same time, women value long-term relationships over someone simply geared to let you in on the latest, fly-by-night stock tip. Women are accordingly more open about their relationships with others, I think, which makes it easier for them to plan for their chosen beneficiaries. So, I must admit, this inspires me to go the extra mile, providing my best level of professional expertise and detailed attention to their retirement solutions. I find it gratifying that they seem to listen closely to my advice. They don't always take it, but we often joke about the way a man can wander the countryside until he's hopelessly lost - only then relenting to ask directions. You find an immediate parallel in financial planning: Women statistically seek out the right kind of expertise in a financial advisor, more so than men in some situations.

Women are more likely to want a roadmap for their *entire* future, rather than a short-term financial horizon. Men are more willing to chance a market loss or two along the way, even if such losses could have tragic consequences on their retirement lifestyles. Yet, I deal with both personalities every day and have done so for decades, often noting that women tend to be less over-confident about having enough money to last a lifetime in retirement. We accordingly spend more time talking about what it means to be "comfortable" in retirement – truly comfortable emotionally versus materially – which comes down to mastering that elusive concept called "true happiness." This is why women find it easier to focus on the most important things in a comprehensive retirement package.

Women "Get It"

I'm saying that women tend to "get it" from the beginning when it comes to understanding the value of guarantees in retirement. It makes a difference. They're more likely to want to draw income from annuities, while some of their male counterparts think they'll somehow survive retirement in the market, even when they know the escalating consequences of risk. So, we're talking about two different mentalities, here, and I understand where men like this are coming from: I can give them guarantees and, if they have enough to live on, I help them participate more actively in market. I just want everyone to know what we're up against.

We've all been through the mill financially. Since the crash, I've become more dedicated than ever when it comes to helping people protect themselves financially. At Reindel Retirement Solutions, we're in the business of minimizing risk while ensuring steady income you cannot outlive and, again, women 'get it.' I wish more men would look beyond the current market and see that they, too, stand to live very long lives in retirement. At a certain age, they need guaranteed principal and income more than anything else.

Women understand that they will live longer than men in retirement – at least six years, or more, statistically, which is a given these days. While 40 years ago, most women let men handle all things financial, including securities and other investments, nearly half of all boomer-generation women queried for a recent report cited knowledge about investing in securities and many reported extensive knowledge, according to a Wharton Financial Institutions Center report.

I've seen a dramatic increase among women who have become keenly interested in the way the market operates. Once they "get it," they show a real passion for preserving their workplace earnings for a safe, guaranteed income stream in retirement. I've been able to help them feel far more confident about having enough income for retirement. Like millions of investors, many women lost retirement savings during the '08 economic meltdown. Since then, the Wharton study indicates that more than 50 percent of women over 65 - from singles to widows - rely on Social Security for their retirement income.

As you've already seen in previous chapters, I have discovered all sorts of ways to really ramp up the "income gap" when it comes to Social Security benefits, knowing that roughly 45 percent of unmarried women rely on Social Security for nearly all of their retirement income.

Women Favor Annuities

An overwhelming percentage of women – more than 70% according to the Wharton study – have a strong preference for fixed annuities with higher lifetime income guarantees, while men prefer annuities with less income and higher potential earnings related to performing markets. Not surprisingly, men favor Fixed Indexed Annuities and I have solutions for both, because women are taking stronger roles in the planning process. This has already led to a striking difference in the financial planning industry. More financially empowered than any generation before them, women in the boomer demographic (born between 1946 and 1964) have adopted stable investment strategies for inheritance from their parents and husbands. This is why financial professionals have begun to take notice. Through the next decade and beyond, women will own more than two-thirds of all U.S. consumer monies as they become heirs to the largest transfer of wealth this country has ever seen – an estimated $12 trillion to $40 trillion, according to a Fleishman-Hillard study of new-business development.

An Exciting Trend for Me!

I'm excited because, if current trends continue, women will introduce a new age of conservatism on Wall Street, and I think we, as a nation, will be better for it. Given this powerful movement, retirement strategies would trend in the logical direction of guaranteed income and principal . . . and that's where I come in!

Here, at Reindel Retirement Solutions, we have always been champions of common-sense planning. We began catering to women long ago, listening to voices of both spouses, loud and clear. Since the last recession, women have been flocking to guaranteed income and principal, which has become more of a priority for investors everywhere. In other words, we're all done with nagging market uncertainty. We want top-quality products from first-rate insurance carriers, along with accurate, no-nonsense answers from first-rate professionals who know their stuff . . . like me!

This is why the numbers of women in my client-base have grown exponentially in recent years. They tend to be avid readers so, not surprisingly, they read my books. They've heard my message loud and clear in past radio broadcasts and seminars. They understand the importance of income guarantees and principal that cannot be lost in erratic market swings. Yes, they really do "get it." And I have long understood the underlying, common-sense financial savvy of women, well before it was recognized in my industry. In fact, I staked my professional future on the emerging power of women in control of wealth, so if you happen to be a woman still intimidated by the financial world, don't be.

Look at the writing on the wall. Know that women have a great sense of financial security and they know how to keep it close to home. Not many people realize that more than half of all Americans with $500,000 or more in assets are *women* (according to IRS analysts). This is why smart-money retirement planners will increasingly focus their attention on women as investors in the coming years. I knew it back when and I'm certain of it now. The antiquated days of "hot-shot" Wall Street Wolverine retirement planning are numbered.

Women place a premium on trust, and they demand respect. They expect the same from an advisor and they get it with me. With roughly 1.3 million women earning in excess of $100,000 a year, the insurance industry has been responding to a new level of consumer demand, and this is one of many reasons we've been growing so quickly at Reindel Retirement Solutions. We work hard to earn trust and respect from our women clients. Here, it's reality, not just talk. We often schedule more meetings with our women clients because they tend to be more meticulous about their retirement plans. They know they can trust my patience and perseverance, which comes from watching the intimidation tactics of certain types of people in my industry. I walked away from all that quickly, in the very beginning of my career. I've always listened closely when wives, widows and working women began to speak because I sensed, way back when, that women had far more insight than stereotypes of the times would allow.

When it came to implementing retirement solutions, I knew that women had much greater influence than most planners realized. Even today, few in my industry realize that women represent the primary market for financial and banking services. This is why I felt compelled to devote a chapter to women as investors and savvy planners, especially when it comes to income and asset preservation in retirement.

This is especially gratifying for me because when it comes to my kind of retirement planning women "get it." We respect each other, I think, because I stand apart from the old male-macho-stereotype market broker. Oh, I can definitely hold my own when it comes to directing market investments, but that's not really what I'm about. I hate watching people lose money. That just about sums it up. I've seen it. I've been there. I can't stand it. My women clients sense it when we meet, and I strongly suspect that my women clients will form an increasingly important presence in the *future* of my business.

I hope every woman in need of an advisor will take a closer look at my personal and professional background. You will find that I am, quite literally, an open book, as they say. But, again, I don't expect you to take my word for it. The following profile comes from another of my clients. In her own words, she 'says it like it is' when talking about what it's like to work with me.

CHAPTER SEVENTEEN

Guarantees in Motion

I'M ABOUT TO *introduce you to someone who - like many women today – has both business and securities-market experience. She has had her share of market ups and downs as well. Yet, like so many women I run into these days, she sensed early on that it was time to begin looking ahead at a real retirement plan, one that would sustain her chosen lifestyle from beginning to end.*

She wanted a plan without the uncertainties so many people face when leaving their assets to the market. She's also like the many women who run their business like they run their finances: with a keen eye on details and future results. As a savvy and experienced business owner and investor, she is well accustomed to the fluctuations of business income and investment returns. She already knew - before she came into my office - that retirement-income fluctuation was precisely what she did NOT want for her retirement income plan.

Like many women today, she also took an active role when it came to retirement planning for herself and her husband. She was not only done with risk for the income side of her portfolio, she was ready to jump in and take charge because she knew the value of guarantees for income and principal. All she needed was an experienced hand to put things in motion, which is why she came to me.

More and more women like her are stepping forward today to make sure their retirement destinies are moving in the right direction. I can safely say that her retirement plan is definitely "in motion" and will soon give her everything she and her husband will need in their retirement years. For the purposes of this book and to protect her identity, her "stage name" is Suzanne:

****

Suzanne:

I'd like to thank David Reindel for giving me the opportunity to say something about retirement planning. Without a doubt, people really need to get involved. As a business owner, I know all too well that your income can not only fluctuate, it can fluctuate a lot. Sometimes you feel like you're investing more into your business than you're getting out of it, and because business valuations sometimes go up or down, as a business owner it can get pretty scary when you look at retirement, wondering if you will ever end up with enough money to retire.

Then I had the same questions I've always applied to my business: Will you ever run out of money? If this happens to a business, you go out of business and that's that. So, what happens once you manage to retire and you run out of money? That's no position to be in, especially not in retirement, so I think it's wonderful that people can plan lifestyles based on enough fixed income to support their accustomed lifestyle.

As the years went on, I became more and more concerned that we would never be in that situation, but then we began working with David. Since then, we've been able to put together a plan that will actually let us retire, and not just retire on food stamps but retire to a lifestyle to which we have become accustomed. Not only that but we can look forward to having an income that will give us enough to live on forever.

We will have all that *and* we will still have all the money we originally invested, our principal investment! Our principal can be passed on as inheritance and to me, this is really exciting. It's very nice to know that you have a real cushion to keep you from going broke before you die, and to keep the people you leave behind from going broke *after* you die, meaning that your surviving loved ones won't have to pay for your funeral, among other things.

As an investor in the market, I've been through all sorts of market ups and downs, including the crash in 2008. But that wasn't the only time the market dropped. Over the course of our lives, my husband and I have definitely lost a ton of money from stocks to oil and gas investments. That's why people begin to question what financial advisors are all about. Some don't always give the best advice. Trust me on that one. A lot of financial planners like to talk about having the right "mix" in a retirement plan full of stocks and mutual funds, but let me tell you something: No matter what kind of mix you have in a retirement plan like that, very few people come out of it without losing a bunch of money.

Then you find yourself wondering where it all went. After all of our gains and losses, my biggest concern was that I would never be able to retire with enough money - not without having to work all sorts of odd jobs. I also knew that we were on a road without a lot of certainties. We had a lot of *un*-certainty.

To get out of that kind of situation, you need to get everything in order and start again. When we went to Dave, we had a very well-organized stack of financial information. We did our best to identify what our monthly budget was at the time, along with other information. Dave was able to take that information and work with it to come up with a plan of action. When he finished, we were able to thoroughly review the plan and by then it was obvious: We definitely needed a guaranteed amount of earned interest and guaranteed preservation of principal. In this day and age, this is not only the way to have a pretty decent retirement lifestyle, it's probably the only way to have certainty in your life.

The other hard-part is to plan ahead when times are good. Things in the market were doing fairly well over the 10 years before the last crash. Back then, you would put your worries aside, based on the idea that if you lose money you'll make it back again. You make a good choice, you win, you make a bad choice and you lose, right?

But as you age, you begin to see that you won't always have all those years ahead for saving. All of a sudden you wake up one day and you're 60 years old, and you don't want to run the rat race you've been running for the last 30 years. You have to do a reality check. You should do something proactive before it's not too late. Unfortunately, some people wait too long.

We all have different ways of dealing with money and we all have different dreams, but here's something I learned in business and then, later, when it came time to planning our retirement: You need to forget about dreams. You must turn your dreams into goals and have real deadlines for reaching those goals – and you need to put it all down on a sheet of paper, otherwise it's all still a dream and nothing more.

We took our dreams and goals and put them into annuities, and I'm very glad we did because I *know* our annuities will take care of us. The annuity provides guaranteed income for life and it's indexed so as the market goes up it can improve, but the base rate will never go down. Basically, the insurance company guarantees a base rate, which can improve when the market improves, and that's the beauty of it.

Amazingly, this kind of answer was right there all along. More and more people need to realize that there are options like this available, and that you don't have to just risk everything in retirement. What I'm saying is that it's great to have a lot of money, but you need more than that, you need a good plan. We had assets in all kinds of things before the last crash and we took one hit after another - until we had to ask ourselves where we were going.

You need to face facts and turn your dreams and fantasies into something you know will be there for you. Again, if it isn't written into a good, working plan, you're just dreaming. So, write it down and develop a smart plan with specific, measurable goals. Maybe you think you have it all together in your brain, but if you haven't mapped it out on paper, you don't know the difference between dreams and reality.

Sometimes I wonder whether people are just afraid to face the reality of where they really are. When it comes to retirement planning, maybe they would rather dream instead. But it just won't work. And let's face it, unless you've been handling money professionally all your life, you need some help, but you need the *right* kind of help. You need help from someone who really understands *retirement*, not just *investment*. We worked with all kinds of planners in the past who gave us nothing but a lot of "ifs." . . . Meaning: "if" this happens, then that "might" happen. This won't cut it, believe me. Keep working with that kind of person and it can become frustrating. You put your money with them but, in the end, you feel that you hardly know them.

At one point, we had our money with a highly recommended financial planner but we weren't very comfortable working with him, nor were we comfortable with the way he was investing our money. After the last crash, and during the recession that seemed to drag on forever, we felt that it was time to take what we had and make the best of it. This meant finding a real *retirement* expert to help us sort it all out. That person was David Reindel.

Before we started working with Dave, we ran through so many options with so many financial people, but in the end we found that they really didn't have a clue. They weren't very well educated in any specific area of the financial world and unless you're working with someone who is, you can wind up in trouble. These people might have taken a couple of courses and passed a couple of tests, but in reality they may be pushing only certain products from certain companies.

You want someone who is strictly independent, not tied into some company like T.D. Ameritrade or Edward Jones. An independent expert can look at everything and find just the right thing. Dave isn't owned by anybody and that is the real beauty in working with him. You still have to do your homework and make sure you know who you're dealing with, but mainly, you need to do it now, not later when things go wrong. Make it a priority and get ahead of all those little crises in life that can and do happen, whether you're ready for them, or not.

✳✳✳✳

I hope you remember Suzanne and what she has to say about life priorities. We've come through a long decade of financial turmoil but we're not done yet. Economic meltdowns are going to be part of the human landscape, no matter how rosy things may seem at any given time. We will always hear "experts" bang the drum for exciting stock tips, distracting us from the reality of things to come. But know this: Today's annuity has come a long way, even in the few years since the Great Recession. People have spoken and they now demand a new generation of instruments that allow them to Make Money without Risking Money. Why not? My only question is this: Why weren't today's wonderful annuities available 30 years ago?

Why has it taken so long for the investment world to catch on to one, basic fact: If you put every investor at risk, everyone risks losing everything . . . leaving nothing more to invest.

The Self-Funded Pension

Investment advisors everywhere learned this the hard way. Their clients never forgot. This is why annuities have become a government-recommended alternative for 401ks and other 'defined contribution' plans. They call modern annuities "the self-funded pension," a replacement for the bygone pensions our grandparents relied upon - the very kind of pension today's radically consolidated company-model can no longer support.

So, we're on our own. And maybe that's a good thing. When it comes to ensuring a life of play instead of work, the art of 'making money without risking money' rules the road to a successful retirement.